YOUR
intentinal
DIFFERENCE

YOUR
intentinal
DIFFERENCE

ONE WORD
CHANGES EVERYTHING

KEN TUCKER
TODD HAHN
SHANE ROBERSON

M·J

NEW YORK

YOUR intentional DIFFERENCE
ONE WORD CHANGES EVERYTHING

Published in New York, New York, by Morgan James Publishing. Morgan James and The Entrepreneurial Publisher are trademarks of Morgan James, LLC. www.MorganJamesPublishing.com

The Morgan James Speakers Group can bring authors to your live event. For more information or to book an event visit The Morgan James Speakers Group at www.TheMorganJamesSpeakersGroup.com.

BitLit
FOR ALL THE BOOKS YOU OWN

FREE eBook edition for your existing eReader with purchase

PRINT NAME ABOVE

For more information, instructions, restrictions, and to register your copy, go to **www.bitlit.ca/readers/register** or use your QR Reader to scan the barcode:

ISBN 978-1-63047-013-5 paperback
ISBN 978-1-63047-014-2 eBook
ISBN 978-1-63047-016-6 hardcover
Library of Congress Control Number:
2013952874

Cover Design by:
Rachel Lopez
www.r2cdesign.com

In an effort to support local communities, raise awareness and funds, Morgan James Publishing donates a percentage of all book sales for the life of each book to Habitat for Humanity Peninsula and Greater Williamsburg.

Get involved today, visit
www.MorganJamesBuilds.com

Habitat
for Humanity®
Peninsula and
Greater Williamsburg
Building Partner

TABLE OF CONTENTS

ACKNOWLEDGEMENTS

We'd like to acknowledge and thank our partners, colleagues and friends at TAG Consulting for their contributions to this book. They've encouraged us personally, embraced these ideas in their work with our clients, and—best of all—are stellar examples of men and women who are living into their Intentional Difference.

Additionally, we want to also acknowledge Jeanna Gregory and the entire Chickasaw Nation Division of Commerce team, including, Sherri Waters, Bill Lance, Pat Neeley, Jennifer Kaneshiro, Dakota Cole, Sharon Darby, Rob Jacks, Bobby Jones, Wayne McCormick and many others for the input, feedback and at times push back as we posited the seminal ideas of *Intentional Difference* as a means to increase productivity and employee engagement.

CHAPTER ONE

What's Your Difference:
YOUR POTENTIAL?

The road up Pikes Peak is riddled with hairpin turns taking you around high-altitude curves, mere inches from the cliff's edge with the turns and twists only getting worse as the altitude increases. Even professional drivers are challenged by a drive up Pikes Peak; the challenges of the road require such a driver to be at his very best every second. You have to be totally focused on the action of driving: all senses fully engaged, never looking off the road and always planning how to navigate each upcoming turn. A miscalculation as you career around a corner, a dip in concentration for even a moment, would be almost certain death. And that's if you are a professional driver.

Now, imagine if you are the head of a research team commissioned by a leading university and an international company to get a car to the top of Pikes Peak. Without a driver.

This was the situation Chris Gerdes found himself in on a September day in 2010. Backed by a multi-million dollar investment from Audi, the car manufacturer, the Stanford professor and his hand-picked team of graduate students had engineered an autonomous—"driverless"—vehicle. And now it faced its first and biggest test: ascending the notorious peak. Lives weren't at stake here: Everything in the car was controlled by computer programming. However, Gerdes's professional reputation—as well as theory, science, even innovation itself—was.

As the drive began, nerves were tense, and the anticipation was high as the car started on its way. All eyes, all senses, all cameras and gear, were in tune and focused on the car.

Suddenly, the car's ascent was interrupted by a thunderous noise. Disaster! The car, Chris's baby, was fine, but the film helicopter that had been recording the momentous event had crashed into the mountain. Unlike the car, that helicopter was staffed by people—victims who were now at great risk.

Talk about an unanticipated development. Talk about a workday going south fast.

"There was this sense of being absolutely stunned, followed by this feeling that nothing else now was as important as getting to the victims," Chris remembers.

The helicopter had crashed at a site so remote that it would take some time for rescue crews to get to it. The only hope of reaching the crash site quickly was to rely on the group of researchers, engineers, and Ph.D. students who were in the lead and chase cars accompanying the autonomous vehicle. In an instant, the mission changed from getting a driverless car to the top of Pikes Peak to saving lives.

In order to fully appreciate how the events of the next hours unfolded, you have to understand more about who Chris Gerdes is and how he built this team. To do this, you need to understand more about Chris's Intentional Difference. Intentional Difference, or ID, is *the purposeful, determined, and productive use of that which is different about you*, but more about this later.

Chris's Intentional Difference showed up early. First, there were the puzzles that fascinated him as a boy. These morphed into computer math programs that he wrote in junior high, back in the days when the school computer took up an entire room! But Chris was not a stereotypical lone ranger computer programmer immersed in online games and eating Cheetos while living in his parents' basement. Chris was different from the popular portrayal of the high school computer geek because he was as engaged by people as he was by computers. In particular, he had always been fascinated by teams and what made the people on teams function at a high level.

Later, Chris served as a residential aide in his dorm while a student at the University of Pennsylvania. One of his duties was supervising security for hundreds of students. Despite his best efforts, he found himself falling behind on the paperwork. He knew he had missed some details when his boss called him in one day.

"I thought for sure I was going to get fired," said Chris. "But then my boss did something I will never forget. He looked at me and said, 'I know you are missing some paperwork, but the thing you are really doing well is building a great team where people get the job done, and are loyal to and cover for each other. I'm giving you more responsibility.'

"I realized up to this point I was evaluating myself on my weaknesses—my failure to do the paperwork, but by doing so, I was missing my strengths."

There was another significant marker in Chris's days as an undergraduate.

"A very close friend was killed in a car crash while we were both students," he explains. "It was obviously hard and tragic on a personal level but it's also impacted my career. I work in vehicle safety now. That's what the autonomous vehicle is all about—not just creating a driverless car because it's cool, but actually being able to make the driving experience safer for people. I've actually never been a really big car fanatic, which surprises people. However, I look back at my friend's death and see how that experience has in some ways led me to work in vehicle safety. I'm not in it to be known for the autonomous vehicle, I just want to improve safety in vehicles."

"I get to combine that goal with my real love, not research, but mentoring students. That and shaping a really compelling classroom and lab experience."

To get there, Chris followed up his undergrad education with business school, also at Penn. He enrolled in a challenging organizational design class where he found his fellow students to be fiercely competitive. He also found an unexpected sense of camaraderie from his like-minded classmates.

"We all got together and I remember saying, 'I want to get an A in this class without busting my ass or kissing anyone else's ass!' We all laughed and decided to collaborate together, which took the pressure off." For Chris, the class turned into another opportunity to learn the benefits of working as a team. "It was really more effective taking the class as a team," he says now. "And the ones who committed to that were the ones who did the best."

It was also at Penn where Chris met a teacher whom he still cites as a lifelong influence, Professor Vijay Kumar, Chair of Mechanical Engineering and Applied Mechanics at the university's School of Engineering and Applied Sciences.

"Vijay is this internationally known engineering and robotics professor—really a very brilliant guy," says Chris. "But there was something different about him. He had this very unselfish, genuine interest in his students and a real belief if you focused on what was right for the students then everything else would fall into place.

"Vijay helped me to see beyond just the technical aspects of the work and to look more specifically at how to motivate the people who were charged with doing the work," says Chris. "He helped me to see that people, not processes or products was the real place where excellence comes from. It was with Vijay's help I began to realize I had a knack for getting people to work together as a team."

After graduation, when it came time to choose a Ph.D. program in engineering, Chris had narrowed it down to two final offers. Both universities offered excellent educations—and sterling credentials. The difference was in the experience they offered, one more than the other offered the opportunity for Chris to express his Intentional Difference.

In retrospect, he now says, the choice was easy: "One school would have just had me as part of a bunch of folks all doing the same thing. The other school would allow me to build my own area." Chris hadn't forgotten the lessons he had learned about building teams—nor had he forgotten that his team-building skills were, indeed, special. He chose the second school: "There, I could help to shape the environment. And I knew I wanted that environment to be all about collaboration."

That decision has marked everything about Chris's career. Fast forward nearly two years to the day after the helicopter crash, and we were driving through the sculpted farmland of Northern California, to visit Chris and his team, who were testing their autonomous vehicle at the Thunderhill Racetrack near Willows. We were there to interview Chris, but the day quickly became more about observing how he leads his team.

This team was quite impressive. Fourteen intensely bright young men and women, talented beyond belief; they were working with hundreds of thousands of dollars worth of high technology equipment. Of course, Chris is quite impressive, too. Brilliant and driven, he was not only in charge of this high-powered team, he was also responsible for the success of an extremely high-stakes project, one that his reputation, his professional future, might depend on.

Let's be blunt. With this kind of mix, you would expect some divas—male and female.

We saw the opposite.

We saw a group of people collaborating, focused on a task. Despite the pressure involved, the high stakes and the obvious intelligence of all the participants—men and women who were probably used to being the smartest people in the room—we never heard anyone trying to take control. We never heard a raised voice. And this wasn't enforced behavior, inflicted from above by an overpowering boss. There was no apparent stress. Unfailingly polite, members suggested solutions to problems that arose, rather than criticizing errors and omissions. They functioned, in other words, as a team.

Most interesting was the way Chris interacted with his team. He is a tenured professor at Stanford University. A man entrusted by car manufacturers with a multimillion-dollar project. A scientist and innovator on the cutting edge of technological developments with the potential to change the very nature of the driving experience in the most profound way since Henry Ford's Model T took over for the horse and carriage.

You'd expect him to be pretty confident in his ability to provide answers.

Instead, Chris had a different, less directive approach to leadership. Instead of giving answers, he asked questions all day long.

A student would approach him with a problem. He would think for a moment and then ask a penetrating question of either that student or the group as a whole. You could see the wheels turn. And then the student or the collective group would suggest a solution and get about executing it.

"This program attracts some really bright people," Chris told us. "But not everyone is right for the team. We had a student once who came to me really bothered by, well, here's how he put it: 'This team cares more about what gets done than how much each person is contributing intellectually, and I'm not sure I'm comfortable with that.'"

Chris laughs as he remembers the conversation. "I told him I was very comfortable with that! We ended up parting ways, because he was never going to buy into the collaborative nature of what we are about."

"My very best days at work are when a student has an idea that moves us forward. It doesn't have to be my idea. As a matter of fact, it usually isn't."

Over lunch at the trackside grill, our conversation turned briefly from the values of teamwork and collaboration to the technical aspects of Chris's work. We asked Chris, "What makes you a good engineer and engineering professor?" Chris thought for a moment, absent-mindedly swatting away flies.

"It's problem-solving, I think. That's what actually gets me up in the morning—the unsolved problem, and figuring it out. I've always loved isolating, understanding, and solving problems."

"In our work we are basically studying how things move. From the data we take from the car after each test drive, we have to deduce what's actually going on. We're like blind guys who are each touching only a part of an elephant. One is touching the tail and another touching the snout, each one arriving at a conclusion based upon a very small part of the whole. I am able to look at specific things and then take a step away and see the whole deal and I just sort of know where to go from there."

Then he shifted to his values and passion again, "It's really more about the students than the research. When people leave the lab I want them to have confidence in their own abilities to find good problems, solve them, and to work with other people."

Think about that for a moment. Most of us dread problems. Chris recognizes and seeks out "good problems." That's different.

The impact Chris's unique "difference" brings to a team was on full display that day on Pikes Peak, when the helicopter crashed.

"At that moment, everything became about the problem of finding the copter and helping the people there. Our team was in the best position to do that, even better than the rescue personnel. No one panicked; everyone was calm."

"The team was so resilient. We sifted through the options and were eventually able to put people in different places and positions—some to communicate with rescue people, others to get people up and down the mountain, some to actually try to find and help the three people in the copter. Everyone just went to work as a team."

Fortunately, everyone aboard the helicopter survived the crash, due surely—in part—to Chris's team performing in such a calm, mission-focused, and collaborative way.

So what is it about Chris that gives him both the desire and ability to build collaborative and effective teams? And why did we start our book with his story?

Because in some ways, Chris's story is your story. Chris possesses a unique difference within him. So do you. He is putting that difference to determined, purposeful, and productive use. So can you. Like Chris, you have a "difference." And that difference represents potential. In fact, you were purposefully made different to make a difference. That's right, your difference is not a deficit! Your difference is *your* potential. Your difference is not a bad thing or something to be suppressed; it is your potential waiting to be unleashed. Potential is defined as an excellence, or an ability that has yet to be developed. For most people their 'difference' is like that–unrealized and undeveloped…and un-intentional. Not so for Chris Gerdes. And hopefully, not so for you.

A Crucible Moment

2010 was, to put it mildly, an interesting year for Chris.

First, there was the helicopter crash during his autonomous vehicle's trek to the top of Pikes Peak.

But even before that there was the Toyota controversy—a major brouhaha that landed his name in national news reports.

Meet Chris and you know he's not an attention-seeker. But attention sought him in the spring of 2010.

There had been a rash of incidents involving vehicles manufactured by Toyota. Media reports were terrifying—the Toyota vehicles were accelerating suddenly, outside the control of the driver—and horrible accidents ensued. The phenomenon was dubbed "sudden acceleration."

The problem was considered so serious that the United States Congress convened to investigate, calling a nationally known professor of mechanical engineering to testify. Without hesitation, he declared that Toyota's engines all incorporated a specific malfunction that could lead to the acceleration. Every owner of a Toyota (and there are lots of them) gasped for breath. The viability of an internationally known corporation teetered on the brink. Maybe it should, millions thought. After all, to build cars that were designed with such a flaw was terrible. An oversight with potentially tragic consequences.

Toyota was understandably concerned—but wasn't yet ready to concede defeat. So the auto manufacturer called in its own experts to evaluate the engineer's findings. Chris Gerdes was one of them. When he received the call, he thought he'd write a report and be done.

Instead, he landed in a media maelstrom.

Chris and other academic experts joined with industry leaders in engineering and discovered the fault-finding professor, in his testing, had added an additional component to the circuitry Toyota had built into its cars. A component that created the sudden acceleration syndrome. A component *not* in Toyota's cars.

So they reported their findings and, because Chris was the speaker at a press conference, he bore the brunt of accusations that he was covering up for the malfeasance of a multinational corporation.

"It was bad science," Chris told us. "And I had a responsibility to stand up and say something. But that had a cost. I had e-mails questioning my integrity, saying I was covering for a big company. But I didn't ask for money from Toyota, so I read these e-mails as questioning both my integrity and my business sense!"

Somehow, he managed to laugh heartily.

"So, here I am, this obscure scientist suddenly having the ear of the top people at Toyota and being called to Congressional hearings. The tension was incredible. It would have been so much easier just to go away. There was no economic incentive to me and a terrible downside, except for my conscience."

"But I have a moral obligation when I see bad science to stand up and say something."

And then Chris said the clincher statement.

"I felt like a character in a novel. Would I do the right thing…or not? Would I stand up and stand alone?"

At this point in the conversation we knew his answer and so do you. But Chris needed to unpack the question—he needed to understand why he was going to do what he was going to do. He needed to understand why—all the reasons why. Why would he most often take the more difficult approach? Why would he take the road less traveled? Why does he go where others would not? What is this difference he possesses?

As we spoke that day, Chris began to wonder, "What is my Intentional Difference?" So we started Chris on the voyage to discover his ID with our idDiscover© process. The result was nothing short of amazingly revealing both for Chris and for us.

You see, the major discovery surrounding Intentional Difference is that our ID can be distilled into one simple idea, expressed in *ONE* word. It takes time and a very carefully calibrated process requiring wise guidance, but it is one that is proven and documented by hundreds of people in our experience.

There is nothing more liberating and clarifying than the journey to discover your ID. And the process is one of almost instant enlightenment: At one moment you are frustrated and pained at how unaware you are of how to put your difference into words. In the next instant the pent up yearning of the soul bursts free as you utter the unique word, your word, which captures your essence. This one word is more revealing of your personhood than any list of labels that others may provide to describe you. And, because this is your idWord, swelling up from within you, one that you name, it does not fade away into disuse after the initial excitement wears off, as often happens with many self-discovery assessments. No, your idWord encompasses the multi-dimensional you. It expresses the difference you bring to your work, relationships and life in general. It describes your consistent and durable identity. It provides a lever that you can intentionally pull to make more of a difference rather than just more of the same. It is this realization that is the one thing that changes everything. It did for Chris Gerdes.

That September afternoon back in 2012, at a racetrack in California, Chris sat down with us to reflect on the key events of his life, his marker moments and his values, as well as his skills and passion. He discovered how to articulate his identity in just one word. And as he reported to us recently, "that discovery, knowing my one word, helps me fine tune and adjust how I challenge and cajole students to reach for the stars."

So what about you? Are you ready to discover your Intentional Difference, or ID for short? Are you ready to further unleash your potential by becoming more intentional with your difference? Read on then, as we begin our voyage to discover your ID together.

CHAPTER TWO

What's Your ID:
YOUR PERSONAL VOYAGE?

Your voyage to discovery begins with understanding that Intentional Difference, your ID, is demonstrated through six dimensions: *Critical Outcome, Driving Passion, Assimilated Experience, Cumulative Knowledge, Emergent Skill, and Prevailing Talent.* These dimensions provide six lenses through which you can understand and observe your difference. Remember Chris Gerdes from the last chapter? Remember how he needed to unpack the why? Why would he most often take the more difficult approach? Why does he go where others would not? What is the difference he possesses?

We helped Chris to answer these questions by having him look at himself through these six dimensions. The result was the discovery of his ID, as captured in his idWord. This book will allow you to do the same—to make the same journey of discovery, to uncover your own Intentional Difference, as captured in your idWord. It will give you answers to help you know more fully who you are, what you are meant to do and how you can be more intentional with your difference. But first let's get started by looking at a brief definition for each dimension:

Critical Outcome

These are the measurable, unique, and notably excellent results you achieve. This is your brand. A brand is something a person or company is known for. It describes what they successfully accomplish over and over again. Marketing experts are paid millions of dollars to capture an individual or company's essence in an image or slogan—in a brand. Your brand is the thing for which your friends and co-workers know they can count on you time and time again.

Driving Passion

This is the thing or things for which you have an intense, energizing appetite that demands action. You may get paid for this or you may not, but even if you are—you would do it for free. This is the thing that raises your heart rate, that makes the hair on the back of your neck stand up, that gives you chills, that makes you weep and pound the table or dance around the room. You cannot *NOT* do this thing. It drives you and you can't get enough of it.

Assimilated Experience

This dimension is the historical perspective that shapes, informs, and directs our behavior. As we move through life we are always accumulating experience—good and bad, triumphant and painful, lessons learned and disasters averted. All of those experiences shape us uniquely as they are assimilated into the fabric of our ID.

Cumulative Knowledge

From our earliest days—even in the womb—we are learning. As we age we are influenced by teachers, experiences, books we have read, courses we take, mentors who invest in us, academic degrees we acquire. There is no limit to our capacity to learn and the places we can draw this knowledge from. What makes this particular dimension part of your ID is that there are certain learning experiences that are "sticky;" they adhere to you and become part of who you are and what you do in a way that they may not for others. Cumulative knowledge is your unique retention and purposeful use of information.

Emergent Skill

All of us have things that we are just naturally good at doing, in many cases remarkable things that just come easy to us. This innate ability—which we call "emergent skill"—is honed and shaped, but the important thing to understand about emergent skill is that we are born with it. It is our innate ability that finds automatic and repeated expression and so is part of our ID.

Prevailing Talent

You are unique. You think, feel, and behave like no one else does. You process information, experience emotion, solve problems, and communicate with others in ways that are all your own. You are so you! We call this sixth dimension prevailing talent, and it is your spontaneous, reliable, and measured pattern of thinking, feeling, and behaving.

These six dimensions work in tandem. Each dimension is as important as the other five. Together they produce the remarkable *you* that others come to know, appreciate and rely upon. Take George for example.

When you hear George laugh, you know he's a teenager. Full of joy about his new driver's license, full of plans for his band, George is bursting with life. Get him talking about girls and see the color rush into his face, even as he ducks his head to let his too-long bangs cover his face. George is a kid: a great, normal kid on the brink of adulthood. Full of cheer, full of spirit. Even his fights with his brother are good-natured—playful shoving matches, wrestling bear hugs on the rug, evoking laughing cries from his brother of, "Mom, George is hitting me again!" George brings a special kind of energy with him. He loves to play, to have fun and to discover new things.

Nowhere is his appetite for discovery more evident than in his wide-ranging love for music across the spectrum, from classical to rock. And, we should add, for all instruments: a natural at the guitar and the bass, George is now teaching himself drums. It's like a switch turns on in his brain when he touches an instrument. It is his *Cumulative Knowledge—the unique retention and purposeful use of information* that is at work, as he instinctively knows how to reproduce the sound playing in his head on the instrument in his hand.

Yet it was when George picked up the cello that the magic happened and George's *Critical Outcome—his unique brand as a musician*—really began to emerge for all to see.

George's mother, Sharon brought a new cello to their home to add to the variety of instruments that George and his siblings would have to play. One evening, not long after the arrival of the cello, the familiy returned home from seeing the movie *The Lord of the Rings*, Mike, George's father, watched in wonder, as George, not yet eight years old began picking out the haunting Celtic theme music on the cello. From that moment on George could not be stopped. His *Driving Passion—the energizing, intense need to take action*—in this instance his need to overcome obstacles, became evident as he developed a voracious appetite to master on the cello each new piece of music he heard.

"With music I just hear something and I can play it," he says, detailing perfectly *the innate, automatic and repeated expression* of his

Emergent Skill. "I can figure out the notes and put them in the right order without even thinking about it, I just do it," says George, now eighteen years old. "I just can't explain what or how I feel when I am making or even listening to music." George says, in words describing *the spontaneous, reliable, and measured pattern of thinking, feeling, and behaving of his Prevailing Talent,* "I feel like I'm being carried on a never-ending wave, it just keeps going and going. I feel like I'm in my zone."

George has this yearning, a demanding appetite for musical expression. In this way, perhaps he is like other teens—*talented* teens—who discover their special ability and become consumed with a need to perfect it.

In another way, he is unlike most other teens. When he was born, George was not expected to live. As an infant in Romania, a country lacking many of our health and social welfare benefits, he was placed in the dubious care of a state-run orphanage.

Then the Dennehy family of Connecticut entered the picture. Devoted to helping differently-abled and special-needs children, Sharon and her husband Mike had three biological children of their own but were looking to add to their family.

They found little George in an awful orphanage, underweight for his age, under a sign warning potential parents that he might not live to adulthood. "Unable to Thrive," the sign said, while the medical chart hanging on his institutional crib warned that he might not last another six months.

Think about that. Being labeled "Unable to Thrive."

A daunting prospect for any parent. Still, the Dennehys took the tiny baby home, making him part of a household of love eventually growing to include eight other adopted children.

They created a space, a safe environment and *an historical perspective* for George *that shaped, informed and directed his behavior—they created an Assimilated Experience*—where he could experiment, discover and determine how to put what is different about him to purposeful and productive use.

By the way, George has no arms. He was born without his upper limbs, the very things you need to play the cello. You can't play the cello without arms, can you?

You can if you are George.

George took what was naturally different about him—his ability to make music– and started to embrace that difference with intentionality. It did not matter that he had no hands or arms to hold a cello—to draw the bow across the strings, he had music in him that he desperately needed to express. So, he found a way to make that happen. He demonstrated *one* of the characteristics we consistently find in successful people—successful people have a compelling need to put their difference to productive use. What about **you**? What is the "difference" in you?

Sharon and Mike's commitment and obedience to the calling upon them and the loving home they provide for George and his siblings make for a great story. But there is even a greater story at play here, one that we may miss completely or one we often overlook. It is the story of *why* humans are made different. It is the story of why *you* are made different.

We believe there is one clear and simple reason why Chris, George, and the others we will mention in this book are made different. And it is the reason why you are made different.

But we caution you, to agree with us is to open your life up to scrutiny and examination as to what have you done with your life so far, and what are you planning to do with the rest of your life.

This is really the question we are asking: What are you *called* to do? For we believe that:

You are made different to make a difference.

But what *is* your difference? *How* are you different?

Are you able to name the 'different" in you and understand how that specifically impacts what you do, feel, say, and produce each day? And what about other people - what does their 'difference" look like? Do successful people have a "*different* different?" This seed thought fueled our research as we investigated if there was a unique 'different'—unique trait(s), that highly successful people possess.

We began studying data from leaders in health care, government, education, the not-for-profit sector, and corporate industries. We looked at these leaders' measurements on a variety of respected, standardized tests, including the Clifton StrengthsFinder©, Myers-Briggs Type Indicator © (MBTI), CoreClarity©, 360-degree feedback, and focus group interviews.

The problem? The data revealed that the leaders in our database are all vastly different. They all have unique combinations of talent themes as revealed by the Clifton StrengthsFinder©. On the MBTI some are introverts and others are extroverts. On the CoreClarity© analysis there are leaders representing each of the twelve archetypes. Whether or not you are familiar with these instruments, you see our point:

Every one of the successful leaders we studied was different from one another!

This finding was at first very disappointing because no one trait emerged as common among leaders. Each leader was different. There was no magic key. Darn it!

And, of course, we should have known that all along, people are different. There is no one exactly like you. You are the ONE, the first and only of your kind, *naturally* original.

So we thought we had it figured out: Could it be that successful people don't share a common trait? That people are successful *because of* their differences? We looked at the data again with that question in mind. We were wrong again.

People are not successful simply *because* they are different. Being different does *not* automatically equate to being successful. The people in our study were all different but not all of them were successful. Many leaders have failed because they are so different from what their organization needed or wanted during the time they were in leadership.

Sigh. Back to the data again. This time we noticed a pattern that we had missed. The measurably successful leaders had one thing in common and—surprising to us—it did have to do with the fact that we are different from one another. BUT it was not simply the "difference" making them successful or unsuccessful as leaders.

These leaders were successful because they put their difference to purposeful, determined, and productive use. In other words, successful leaders were *intentional* with their difference. And that intentionality made *all* the difference in their ability to lead well! Chris Gerdes, whom we introduced in the last chapter, demonstrates this kind of intentionality as he leads his team of scientists.

"That's Marie," Chris said pointing out a twenty-something student, "She is brilliant, she successfully finished her Ph.D. two weeks ago, and she will be moving on soon. One of the large technology firms just hired her. That's what I see my class, this work as: as an incubator for new ideas and new idea-creators. Many students discover by doing this research who they are and what they are meant to do. They start off clueless as to what they really want to do. But over the months, with a little guidance and carefully placed questions, each student discovers their niche, their unique area of focus. I am constantly amazed how that is usually the case, especially since each student is so different."

Being different is *so* us as humans, right? Yet, at the same time it is not *us*. Not in practice. We do not *practice* being different. In our daily lives, often we do the opposite and go to great lengths *not* to be singled out as "being different." We try not to be noticed as being unusual. That's what junior high is all about, right—fitting in?

We often default to being just like everyone else rather than intentionally using our difference to excel.

Ah, but the most successful people in our database took a risk to discover, embrace, and repeatedly employ their difference to make an impact on their environments. The common denominator for effective leaders in our database is that *successful people put to good and productive use that which is different about them.*

Stop. Think about that a moment.

We have—and not just for a moment but for a long time.

The idea of Intentional Difference, the process and concept has been germinating for us for fifteen years. Between the three of us, we have 65 years of collective experience studying and practicing in the field of individual and organizational performance. We have consulted with individuals and corporate clients of all types—multi-national corporations, Fortune 500 firms, federal and local government agencies, small companies, health care concerns, and not-for-profit organizations. Through intimate interaction with these diverse leaders and organizations focusing specifically on how to *identify potential,* how to turn that *potential into performance,* how to create environments where *performance becomes practice,* and how to design structures where *practice leads to profitable outcomes,* we have drawn from our experience to make the following observations:

The vast majority—roughly 85%—of what you are capable of doing most anyone can do (please don't be insulted!). Think about it: are you really the only one, or even the only one in your company, who can host a meeting? Who can crunch the numbers? Or even write up a problematic situation so that it sounds like an exciting challenge rather than a dreaded duty?

It's not that those things are not important. They may be part of your job description, and you may have to do them regularly in order to fulfill your role, in order to make your company function. But the skills to complete these tasks—no matter how necessary they may be—are not unique to you; they do not emerge from what makes you different. As a result, these activities—these duties, if you will—do not elicit passion or full engagement from you. You may feel compelled to do these things, but the fact is there are others who naturally perform these activities with much greater effectiveness than you do.

A much smaller percentage—say 10%—of what you are capable of doing select others can be trained and deployed to do. These include highly skilled tasks, maybe even tasks for which you have trained. Creating that job-specific spreadsheet, for example. Or even motivating the sales team to tackle a particularly challenging quarter.

These activities may elicit a very high output from you. They may draw on your creativity, and you may perform them with excellence. However, you execute them based upon your technical knowledge or deep industry experience, based on something you've learned— something you've been trained or trained yourself to do. The fact is, there are others who could be trained to do them just as well. These tasks are not spontaneous for you. You have little to no passion when doing them. You do them when called upon to do so. These activities are still not hitting that sweet spot for you.

Five percent of what you are capable of doing, however, is different. Five percent of what you are capable of doing only you can do—or only you can do in the way you do it.

This 5% is the capacity from which you contribute uniquely, the invigorating well from which you draw when you are doing things at which you are remarkably, amazingly effective. This is what spurs Chris and his approach to teaching students, George and his musical artistry. This is the source from which you draw life and joy, the space where you are doing what only you can do. The special ingredient that adds incredible value in your professional, personal, creative, and volunteer lives.

This 5% is your Intentional Difference! Your I.D. (We will use these terms, your 5% and your ID, interchangeably throughout this book.) It is what makes you special, the essential ingredient that you can utilize to optimize your life. But the tragic fact is that most of us spend most of our time mired in the 85%.

The rote bullet points on a job description.

The routine tasks.

The tasks that anyone else or almost anyone else could be doing instead of you. The things that demand to be done.

This is crazy! Why would we be spending most of our time NOT doing the 5% of the things that we are best at and love doing?

Well, for one thing there are a lot of forces conspiring against us. As we write we are in a tough economy, and most people are just glad to have a job. The prevailing mentality is: "keep my head down, keep my nose to the grindstone, do everything that is asked of me and *then some* so I can pay my bills and feed my family."

For another thing, most of us have never reckoned with the idea of ID and our 5% so we are unable to be intentional around it.

Just so you will know, we understand these factors. We live in the "real world," too. But it doesn't matter—not if you want to do more than survive. Not if you want to thrive. And with that in mind, we are taking a stand. Here and now, we are declaring war on both of those limiting factors—on *anything* that holds us back from tapping our greatest source of power. Regardless of the economy, you will be most valuable as an employee or leader when you are functioning in your 5%—utilizing that which is most special and most valuable in you. Our mission in this book is to help you discover, optimize, and begin to unleash your 5%. People who are purposeful and determined to use their difference in a productive way make a noticeable impact on their surrounding world. They feel exponentially more alive and make a significant contribution because of their difference.

What is the quality of your contributions? Are you contributing from what makes you unique (your 5%) and thereby bringing special value to your organization and relationships? Are you operating within your Intentional Difference? Do you know how your ID improves your interpersonal relationships? Are you using your ID to fine-tune the tasks you spend your time doing? Do you know how your ID improves your contribution to your team? Is your understanding of your ID improving communication effectiveness in your workplace?

These are the questions we answer in this book. To do so, in the first few chapters we help you define and apply the dimensions of your Intentional Difference. In the latter part of the book we will help you begin to optimize and unleash your Intentional Difference.

So, how about it? Do you want to be different—intentionally, observably and unabashedly different? Then read on to learn how to live and work daily within *your (5%) your* ID!

Video in English   Video in Spanish
(http://bit.ly/UxEMFx)   (http://bit.ly/14Arsbl)

Once you have a QR code reader,
place your smart phone over the QR code above.

CHAPTER THREE

What's Your ID:

YOUR CRITICAL OUTCOME?

Have you ever gone fishing? Why do you go?

Many who go fishing say they go for the relaxation. Others go for the thrill of the first hit on the line. Still others go for the quiet solitude. And, then, there are some who fish for entirely different reasons.

You've probably never heard of him, but there is an extraordinary fisherman by the name of Renato Grbic who works the waters of the Danube River in Belgrade, Serbia. Shaven-headed, tattooed, and athletically fit, the 51-year-old Grbic, has a friendy face and a firm handshake. What's most interesting about Renato is that his main preoccupation is not fish, but people. You've got to hear his story.

Fifteen years ago, Renato was fishing under the Pancevo Bridge when he heard a splash behind him. It was a "jumper," one of many people who attempt suicide every year by jumping off this bridge into the cold and turbulent waters of the Danube. Renato didn't hesitate.

He motored over, pulled the man out of the freezing waters, and saved his life. "Such a glorious day and you want to kill yourself!" he told the trembling man. He wrapped the man in his own coat and took him to shore. He brought him to safety—and by reaching out to that poor man in his moment of need, he gave the jumper hope. Life was not meaningless. Somebody cared. Renato gave that would-be suicide a reason to live.

Since that day, Renato has saved 25 other would-be suicide victims, asking for nothing in return. He feels great satisfaction as he carries out his mission of saving others. He's developed a repeatable process. He knows the time of year, the time of day, and the exact locations where people are most likely to jump. Even when it interferes with his actual livelihood—fishing—Renato makes a point of being there. He's committed to being the person who can stop this awful act of desperation. The one man who can change these lives, who can give these people their own life back. In Belgrade, he is called the "Superman of the Danube" and was hailed as a hero by the city's government.

Renato is known for saving lives. He's perfected the process. He does it time and time again. 'Life-saver of the Danube' has become his 'brand.' It is his Critical Outcome. It is what he is known for.

What are you known for? What is it that others have come to expect from you? Take a moment to write down your answer in the box provided. Go ahead, we'll wait.

Your Critical Outcome is our term for your _measurable, unique, consistent, and notably excellent results._ Your Critical Outcome is your personal brand.

What, exactly, do we mean by 'brand' again? Let's think of a few famous examples.

Nike's relentlessly competitive, no-excuses-allowed ethos is captured in the brand slogan "Just do it."

Apple captured its two imperatives— "never stop thinking smarter and better" and "always be differentiated" in the slogan "Think Different." (Notice that it is not "Think Differently," which—while being grammatically correct—would imply something else entirely.)

American Express is known for exceptional and immediate customer service no matter where a cardholder is traveling and so they can say with confidence "Never leave home without it."

And it's not just companies. As we have already noted, people have brands, too.

The mom who always knows just the right thing to do for a fretful child is known as a comforter.

The soup-kitchen volunteer who always makes each client feel like a valued person and not a charity case is known as an encourager.

The Girl Scout leader who encourages young girls to get past societal definitions of "pretty" and to embrace her inner beauty is known for her ability to inspire young women.

The sales professional who always leads the pack and beats quota is known as the rainmaker.

The community leader who always tells the truth, even when it hurts and may cost him status is known as a man of integrity.

The pediatric occupational therapist known as the "child whisperer," who soothingly calms traumatized children.

Think of a few famous people, or just people you know well. What are they known for? What would you say is their brand?

YOU have a personal brand, a Critical Outcome, as well. Are you ready to discover and embrace it?

Let's start by unpacking our definition: Critical Outcome is *your measurable, unique, consistent, and notably excellent results.*

You read that right—your Critical Outcome is *measurable.* This means that you can count, rate, or rank the results you get. Your margins are lower. Your commissions are higher. There are dozens of kids who point to you as "the most influential teacher of my life."

Your Critical Outcome is *unique.* Remember, you are so you! So your results will carry something of your essence in them. You will not be known just as someone who encourages others, but as one whose "brand" of encouraging specifically targets an individual's strengths and helps that person to take one action daily to expand the use of her or his strengths. Many people are great salespeople, but through your brand of "selling," you become a trusted partner with your clients, someone they ask enthusiastically for products and services.

Many people can crochet. But your brand means that you use fifteen cents of every dollar you make from your crochet business to micro-finance organizations in Africa to help other women start crocheting businesses.

Your Critical Outcome is *consistent*. You deliver the same high standard of results again and again. Friends, family members, and coworkers know they can count on you. They will say things like, "If we give Gretchen this seemingly impossible problem, she will develop an elegant solution every single time," or "The one thing you can always count on Bob for is to get people who are at odds to play nice with each other and end up getting great results."

Finally, your Critical Outcome leads to *notably excellent results*. We're not talking about the stuff you are good at, good enough at, or adequate for. You are <u>exceptionally</u> good at this—and sometimes you wonder why everyone else can't produce the same results as you. "I don't get why this is so hard for some people," you say to yourself. "This comes so easily to me. Doesn't it for everyone?" (The answer, of course, is "no.")

Michael Jordan was "notably excellent" in his clutch performance at the end of close basketball games.

Apple, founded by Steve Jobs, consistently creates innovative products with exceptional quality.

Mother Teresa reached into forgotten communities and organized centers to help people in these communities suffering from disease, malnutrition, and poverty. She helped the world see that the Untouchable caste in India was made up of people who needed and deserved our help and attention. Each of these individuals produced excellent results.

Your Critical Outcome is the thing you are known for; it is the lasting impression you leave on others. It is the measurable, unique, consistent and noticeably excellent results ***you*** produce.

Jeff's Story

One of the extraordinary people we interviewed for this book was Jeff Hussey.

Jeff may not be a household name, but he has had an outsized effect on the world of information technology.

A serial entrepreneur, Jeff got an early start. As a young child, encouraged by his mom and dad, he was selling greeting cards and soap door to door. He did these things, rather than take the more conventional childhood jobs of running a paper route or operating a lemonade stand, because "all of the other kids were doing those conventional things."

Jeff felt he needed to individualize his approach to work as well as develop a solution that would benefit his neighbors. He determined that "Everyone needs soap and everyone needs cards for birthdays and special holidays." So he learned the neighborhood's soap and greeting card needs, then built an inventory with those products, developed a sales pitch and became wildly successful with his neighbors as customers.

As a young man, Jeff worked an "impossible" sales route for a business information management company. Faced with an infertile territory, Jeff developed an ingenious strategy to sell computer access and business data more efficiently. Within a couple of months, Jeff had doubled his customer base. Problem was, his ingenious strategy got him fired.

"I basically hacked our existing system to serve our customers more effectively," he remembers. "I knew it was a big risk, but they gave me an impossible problem and I had to solve it. When I did the company fired me because they thought my solution was inappropriate."

Here he pauses, with a gleam in his eye. "I wasn't particularly sad about losing the job, except for the fact I now had no income."

Jeff had been getting into the office before anyone else mining the company resources for business information in those early morning hours and then nailing his sales quota during normal working hours. The worst part of losing his job, besides having no income, was losing access to the data he needed for his investing strategies. Basically, Jeff never saw himself primarily as an employee. He had been thinking about the job as an entrepreneurial opportunity—looking at ways to use everything at his disposal to succeed. Looking at ways to use all the information at his disposal. He may have broken company rules, but he did so in order to perform the job that the company had hired him to do. And his firing— while inconvenient—freed him to follow his true self.

This was back in the mid-1990s, when the Internet was still young. But even then, Jeff had ideas about where this new technology would go. He foresaw that traffic on the Internet was going to grow rapidly and that network server capacity to move this increasing amount of information from one place to another was going to be wholly inadequate.

Let's pause for a moment. *Jeff* envisioned this but, at this point, hardly anyone else did. At this point there was plenty of server capacity. Not every business was on the Internet. But Jeff took a risk, believing the Internet would transform business practices and needs, entirely. So he chose to act on his instinct and began looking for ways to be the one to supply those needs. (Remember this is the kid who figured out how to turn his neighbors into customers for specialty products!)

Jeff looked at what was happening and saw what was coming: more and more business would move to the Internet. As traffic on the Internet grew, Jeff realized, either more servers or faster ones —or both—would be required to sustain it. The problem at that point, in the mid-nineties, was to get twice the speed as a regular server, a business had to pay five times as much. But if traffic grew the way Jeff thought it would, this wouldn't be a negotiable cost—more and faster Internet would become a necessity. Without enough servers a company would lose data, frustrate customers, and forfeit opportunities. This wasn't a problem then—but it was one Jeff saw coming. Basically, he foresaw that the Internet would eventually need an air traffic controller. He gambled everything on the belief that he was right.

It took work—specifically, months and months of begging for startup capital. Not everyone had the foresight Jeff did. But in 1997, he launched a company called F5 Networks. Its signature product, The Big-IP, would be a software solution that searched servers to find light use and open space and direct business networks to those places so their operations could continue without being slowed or stopped.

Here was Jeff's question: "Why don't we just build a gizmo to divide this traffic up between a bunch of cheap servers?"

Just like air traffic controllers direct planes to available air space and empty gates, why not a technology that guides data and information to open spaces on existing servers? That was it—the whole idea. "Someone else was going to do it even if I didn't. So I figured I would" Jeff said, with a shrug of his shoulders.

His timing was impeccable. Business use of the Internet exploded as the dot.com boom transformed American capitalism. Within a few years, Jeff took his company public, hired a new CEO who knew how to manage an exploding business and deftly navigated the dot.com bubble burst, without a negative impact to his bottom line.

And savored his success.

Jeff the entrepreneur moved on to other ventures—advising high capacity investors, funding the development of a phone and computer app that helps people get health care more readily and finding ways to do what he calls his "mission in life"– solve the world's clean water problem.

Though Jeff's initial attempts have been lucrative, his road has not been entirely smooth. He's gone bankrupt twice and endured a measure of personal hardship. There were a few months as the dot.com bubble was bursting when F5's survival was on the line.

But, at the end of the day Jeff is a success. Fertile ground for us to mine an instructive Critical Outcome. This would be easy, right?

Your Critical Outcome? | 33

At first, we thought Jeff's Critical Outcome was surely 'repeatedly creating wealth'. For he has done this multiple times, even through bankruptcies.

But, see, other people have done this too. It's not unique enough to be Jeff's Critical Outcome.

OK, we thought, here it is—the ability to sustain an incredibly high tolerance for risk, even when others can't.

Well, this was certainly true, but there were a lot of risk-taking entrepreneurs in the 1990's and early 2000's in the information technology business.

How about this - the knack for seeing around the corner to understand the 'next big thing'? Again, true. And, again, not unique enough. Remember, Jeff said "Someone else was going to do this if I didn't."

We puzzled and ruminated for months.

All of a sudden, it hit us! Jeff's ID, and his Critical Outcome, had nothing to do with his technological ability, his vision for the future, or his high tolerance for risk. It had everything to do with a dinner we shared at his home in Jackson Hole, Wyoming.

Here's what we mean…

The pivotal conversation with Jeff took place in his magnificently appointed home, where he lives with his teenage son. He invited us there and even prepared a wonderful dinner for us (talk about a gracious host!). As Jeff chopped vegetables, prepared a perfect Chicken Marsala, and shared a wonderfully aged bottle of red wine from his cellar, the breathtaking panoramic view of the Grand Tetons from his dining room window threatened to distract us all.

During our conversation, Jeff briefly mentioned the influence of his father on his life. We scribbled this in our notes and then forgot about it. In that conversation, Jeff shared, "My dad knows almost nothing about business or technology but he knows a lot about people. And the reason he does is because he is great at asking questions. Basically, my dad taught me a weapons-grade version of the Socratic Method." (This is a method of learning that emphasizes drilling down deep into questions instead of trying to come to a quick answer).

This is a method that Jeff is passing along.

"As I have raised my kid," he says, "I have been intentional about asking him: 'Did you ask any good questions today?'"

That's it. The one thing Jeff Hussey does over and over again, is ask good questions. Questions, that are measurable, unique, consistent, and notably excellent. Here are just a few:

What should I do that will set me apart from the other kids on the block?
What innovations would result in better service for my customers in this infertile market?
What does the Internet mean for the future of business?
What is no one else doing when it comes to networking?
Why is no one else doing it?
What would it take for me to do it?
What's next?

Do you see it? Sure, Jeff has created wealth, but he also lost it. Sure, he has an inordinate appetite for risk. Sure, he is a visionary entrepreneur. But underlining all of those things is his ability to ask just the right questions so that he arrives at the best solutions. This is his personal brand. This is his Critical Outcome!

Now, How About You?

Jeff Hussey's story is fascinating and instructive but this book is about YOUR Intentional Difference.

You don't have to be a gifted software entrepreneur. Asking questions doesn't have to be your thing. Your Critical Outcome may have nothing to do with business. But you do have to know your Critical Outcome—everyone does—and it is very likely your own Critical Outcome is something very different than Jeff Hussey's.

So, what are those things for you? What are the unique, measurable, consistent, and notably excellent results you see again and again in your life? What's your personal brand? What are you known for?

Below is an exercise to help you get at the answers to those questions. You can choose to do it now or continue reading onto the next chapter and come back to the exercise later.

Application: Understanding Your Critical Outcome
We call it the *Ten Adjectives* exercise.

First, make a list of words that others use to describe you:

1. _____

2. _____

3. _____

4. _____

5. _____

6. _____

7. _____

8. _____

9. _____

10. _____

Next, take this exercise outside yourself. Find two people who know you well and ask them to add to your list. Fill in their words below. You can do this right now—maybe all you need is a phone call, a text, or an email:

_____

_____

_____

_____

_____

Consider both lists—your original 10 words and the words that your friends added. Circle the three words resonating with you the most. Go with your first instincts.

Write those three words below:

1. _____

2. _____

3. _____

You now have three strong words that are very descriptive of you.

Use the space below to reflect on how those three words are manifested and measured in you. How do others experience these words in you? Be as specific as you can.

Having done this exercise, you are well on your way to not only to clarifying your Critical Outcome, but also we have made our first landfall on the voyage to discover your ID.

CHAPTER FOUR

What's Your ID:

YOUR DRIVING PASSION?

As we learned in the last chapter, Critical Outcome is what you are known for, what people have come to expect from you, the exceptional result you consistently produce. But why this outcome from *you*? What motivates you to produce this specific, unique, and notably excellent result? What do you feel deeply about?

There are specific things that trigger your emotions, fire up your desire, and spur you to give your very best performance. From Michelangelo and the Sistine Chapel, to the imprisoned South African lawyer and the quest to end Apartheid, to the teenage computer geek and the hunger that drove him to create worldwide social interaction, historically, excellence in human performance is fueled by a driving

38

passion. Driving Passion, our second dimension, is *the energizing, intense appetite that demands action*. What is your Driving Passion? Can you articulate it?

At the end of the movie *Serendipity*, one of the main characters makes this statement: "The Greeks did not write obituaries. They simply asked, 'For what did he have passion?'" This philosophy of the ancient Greeks suggests they viewed passion as a way of measuring what a person deemed important enough to spend his life on. In this way, Greek thinkers believed by looking back on a person's life, one could easily see the mile markers that outlined their life's course—distinct instances that revealed their driving passion.

This is a reasonable observation on the part of the Greeks since passion that drives a person to take action is noticeable and identifiable by others. Humans have a built-in radar for passion. We know when a speaker is passionate about her subject or not. We know when a fundraiser has real passion for the cause or is simply after the money. We know when a healthcare provider has a passion for healing, versus being merely enamored with his or her own sense of importance. Our internal passion-sensor is finely tuned to gauge the passion that drives others to action. But what are *you* driven to do that sets off the passion alarm in others? When was the last time someone's action set off your passion alarm?

Ken's passion alarm was set off recently during a business trip. Here's what happened:

I was resting comfortably in my hotel room in Monterrey, Mexico, when the phone rang. The front desk clerk informed me that Lucio Villarreal Garcia was there to see me and could I please come down to the lobby. "Who?" I asked. She repeated the name and added, "He is a taxi driver." Hearing that, I agreed to come down to meet him, thinking that maybe I had left something behind in the taxi I had taken to the hotel earlier that afternoon.

What happened next left an indelible impression upon me and illustrates perfectly the tell-tale presence of a person's Driving Passion. As I began talking with Lucio, my broken Spanish led me to believe he was saying I owed him 20 pesos more for my earlier trip. I was stunned and somewhat irritated. I just could not believe he had come back hours later to get me out of bed, and demand I pay him 20 more pesos—less than two U.S. dollars, and probably less than I had tipped him on the long ride from the airport. Happily, I was wrong.

My verbs and subject were all mixed up. What he *was* saying, was he realized he had miscalculated and charged me 20 pesos too much, so he was returning the money to me. I was stunned. My passion sensor started buzzing in my head. I was curious to know more about what would drive a person to take the actions Lucio Villareal Garcia took to get my money back to me. So once he left, I asked Gracelia, the clerk who had translated for me, about him. She was more than happy to tell me.

I heard from her multiple instances of Lucio returning cameras and wallets with cash and credit cards intact that had been left in his taxi. She also told me of examples of him doing acts of kindness for non-guests as well, including instances of him paying the taxi fare for employees who needed a ride but had no money. Can you imagine that…a cabbie voluntarily paying the fare for a passenger! Lucio's brand—his penchant for going above and beyond for his customers—is fueled by his Driving Passion—*an energizing intense appetite to serve others*. This is his internal motivator, his fuel, pushing him to act in a generous, selfless way that people have come to expect of him. Because of this, I hired him again and again to take me around for the rest of my trip, and I have already booked his services for my upcoming return trips.

I know I can trust Lucio, because I know what drives him.

So what drives you? What do people expect from you? What is the feeling that compels you to act? What do you do that alerts others to the passion that drives you? To answer these questions and help you articulate your Driving Passion lets look at our definition through each of its components:

Driving Passion is *energizing.*

Take, for example, the case of Jeff Olszewski. Jeff is the Chief Financial Officer at ACICS, a college accreditation organization serving hundreds of colleges both in the US and around the world. Jeff is an analytical, accurate, and respected accountant. He has received awards and letters of commendations for his meticulous and flawless audits. One day, as we were sitting in his office on the ninth floor overlooking Union Station in Washington, DC, we asked Jeff, "What energizes you?" He paused a moment, looked down in deep concentration, adjusted his eyeglasses, looked up and said, "I get energy from fixing things—I am most energized when I am wrestling to find a solution."

To illustrate his point, he told us this story. "I enjoy my job doing the rudimentary activities of accounting and finance. But, the most enjoyable time I have had as CFO was a few years ago when we were re-modeling our offices. I was selected to be the onsite project manager for our company to ensure the accurate and timely completion of the construction. It was hard work. The early and long hours along with the daily things that did not go as planned made for a very challenging six months. But, I loved every minute of it. I was in my 'sweet spot.' I went home each day tired but fired up to get back to the site the next day. I was both happy and sad when the project was completed under-budget and two weeks prior to the deadline. I was happy the various teams had worked through multiple instances of seemingly impossible technology and structural challenges in order to complete the construction. I was sad as the range and frequency of unexpected problems and the incessant demand upon me for creative solutions abruptly decreased. My energy and sense of fulfillment has not been the same since," he said. And then he added, almost as an afterthought, "that is, except on weekends."

"On weekends? What are you doing on weekends?" The question was natural.

Jeff, breaking into a smile, replied, "Weekends, I make customized pens from a variety of natural woods." Smiling wider, a glint in his eyes, Jeff went on to explain, "Woods like mahogany and balsa have a beautiful grain that, once polished, make exquisite pens. Problem is these woods are very difficult to work with; they tend to split and crack if you do not apply just the right amount of pressure when you are turning them on the lathe. Each piece of wood is different, so you have to figure out how to best work with one piece versus the other. It takes long hours of concentration and creativity. For me, it's the process of transforming a rough piece of wood into a beautiful, unique, and personal item for each person that drives me forward. It's the process and progress of creating something new that energizes me."

And that was it. Jeff may be known in the wider world as an accountant. He may have earned professional respect and laurels. But his Driving Passion? Making one-of-a-kind pens of both beauty and utility—he is energized by, and has an intense appetite to use his hands and imagination to create objects that are both useful and aesthetic.

What energizes *you*? What activity fires you up? What infuses you with vim and vigor? What gets you out of bed in the morning, gets your heart racing, gets you through the daily slog?

Whatever it is, it is merely thinking of that thing that drives you, brings you to life. And when you have the opportunity to operate in your Driving Passion—wow!

No matter how tired you are, how frustrated you may be in other areas of life, you feel an incredible sense of energy and renewal and joy. This is the thing you are passionate about. And it energizes you!

Driving Passion is an *intense appetite*.

Much like the famous children's story, *The Little Engine That Could*, Ángel Macías and his 1957 Little League teammates, were the *little team* that could.

Ángel Macías was only 12 years old, only 5 feet tall, and 88 pounds in 1957, when he and other neighborhood boys were introduced to the game of baseball by César Faz. The boys—all from the rural town of Monterrey, Mexico—were instructed by Faz on how to build a baseball diamond. They cleared rocks and glass from a dirt field, making bases from old potato sacks. They had one baseball, a bat and homemade gloves. None of the them played baseball before, but they quickly developed an appetite and ability for the game. This did not go unnoticed by Coach Faz, so he applied for and succeeded in getting his team on the roster in the Industrial Little League of Monterrey, Nuevo León.

Within weeks the team was playing and winning against the other three teams in the league. Then in July 1957, Coach Faz's team was invited to play in an area tournament in McAllen, Texas against a team from New Mexico. No one expected them to win. They did not expect to win either. They expected to play one day, lose, and then spend the next two days sightseeing before retuning home. In actuality it would be two months before they returned to Monterrey. Special arrangements were made with the US immigration department for their team visas to last until they were eliminated from the competition. They never were. They won that first game in McAllen 9-2.

Led by ambidextrous pitcher Ángel Macías, the team went on to win six tournaments, including the South Region Tournament, which gave them a berth to play in the Little League World Series in Williamsport, Pennsylvania. Upon arriving in Williamsport, Ángel and his teammates were immediately reminded of the enormity of the task they faced. As is customary, the team was given new uniforms with "South" across the chest, emblematic of their regional championship.

The problem was that none of the uniforms fit. The Monterrey boys were too small. The uniforms were made with a heavier, taller American teenager in mind. The Monterrey boys averaged 4 feet 11 inches and 92 pounds while the US boys averaged 5 feet 4 inches and 127 pounds. The contrast was stark! The team became known as los pequeños gigantes ("the little giants"). And just like the little engine that could, this scrawny team led by Ángel, achieved greater success than anyone ever imagined.

On August 23, 1957, 10,000 fans in the Williamsport stadium and millions of others listening by radio experienced the Driving Passion of an 88-pound 'giant'. Striking out eleven batters, and retiring the remaining seven with pinpoint control, keeping the La Mesa team (who were up to this point in the series were undefeated) from hitting a single ball to the outfield, Ángel Macías did the unprecedented.

That day, he pitched the only perfect game in Little League World Series history. Ángel Macías is one of a kind.

Recently we sat down to interview this history-maker at his home in Monterrey, Mexico. As we sipped iced-tea in his study, we were surrounded by baseball memorabilia, numerous academic and athletic awards and photos of him with two American presidents. Ángel, although retired for thirty years, still has an athletic build, a reminder that after his early stardom, he went on to play and coach professional baseball both in the US and at home in Mexico.

We started by asking Ángel an open-ended question: "Tell us what stands out in your memory about that time six decades ago." He replied, "I remember we loved to play baseball. Each time the ball was hit was sheer delight for us. Winning was not the driver for us; playing the game was. We did not think about beating the other team as much as we thought about perfecting our hitting, running, throwing and catching."

"When we won a game, we savored not the win but the plays that we executed well. In the 1957 Little League World Series, we were the underdogs, the most unlikely team to win—outmatched by the stronger, taller and more experienced US teams, none of whom saw us as a serious threat—but we were hungry, not to win, but to play good baseball. And that was the hunger that drove us."

"What about you? There you were a twelve-year-old with tremendous pressure on you to win, what were you feeling? What was it that you wanted?"

He didn't hesitate to answer. Arms folded, muscles rippling, he said, "I wanted to improve my game, and I saw each new batter as an opportunity to fine-tune my pitch. My appetite to pitch better and better was insatiable."

"So what about your historical perfect game?" we asked.

"I did not set out to pitch a perfect game. I was just pitching to get the other side out. My coach and teammates were aware of the score and that my pitching had resulted in no hits, no runs, no errors and no walks—the perfect game. However, they made sure no one told me. I did not know or at that time much cared about pitching the perfect game." Ángel did pitch the perfect game, the only one in Little League history, and one of 23 in the entire history of both Little League and professional baseball combined. "So," we asked Ángel, "What life lesson did you learn from that experience?"

"I learned desire is an important part of success. The bigger the hunger, the more likely you are to put in the work to succeed. I spent at least four hours every day throwing a ball. I could not help myself. There was this deep down yearning that drove me to do it. I am glad I did—for it is that same internal drive, that intense hunger to get better with each successive attempt, that has paid off for me in my adult life in professional baseball and beyond."

What do *you* have an intense appetite for? What do you yearn to do? What compels you to act?

Driving Passion *demands action*.

It's not imaginary or theoretical or hypothetical. You actually get out there and do stuff as a result of your Driving Passion. You love an orphan, you swing a club, you tutor a kid, you close a sale, you compete in an online video game, you spend time with a senior adult—all because you can't NOT do it. So now you know what Driving Passion is, but how can you know when yours is activated?

There are several indicators that can help point you to when you are operating within your Driving Passion. Just like a detective will follow the clues to get to the solution of the case he is working, so can you follow these indicators to discover your Driving Passion. We call these clues the Three Indicators.

Indicator Number One is *Emotion*.

What makes you so excited that you pound the table? What makes tears well up in your eyes? What sends chills up your spine and raises goose bumps on your arms? What makes you sad, what makes you pump your fist, what makes you laugh, what makes you want to hug a child or adopt a puppy?

Whatever stirs the deepest part of you and makes you want to act, even in ways you would not otherwise have suspected, is clue number one. Think about the things that make you emotional—that make you bark in anger, shiver for joy, laugh outrageously, brush away tears for reasons you don't understand. Whatever makes you highly emotional can help you discover your Driving Passion.

What makes you emotional?

Emotions are beautiful. They are profound, driving, and occasionally dangerous—powerful, innate responses to the world around us. When we see them for what they are—indicators of our heart's deepest yearnings—they can be wise and instructive teachers for us. In the context of our Driving Passion and our Intentional Difference, they are key indicators, like an exit sign when we are confused on the highway or a "Check Engine" light when we are wondering why our car feels like it is running rough. Emotions are key to your Driving Passion.

Indicator number two is *Physical Reaction.*

Our mind and body are intimately interconnected. One of the best ways of understanding what is going on in our mind and heart is assessing what is happening in our body. A physical reaction may be directly connected to discerning your Driving Passion because we experience our strongest, most primal reactions in our bodies. We react to excitement by breathing faster. Our pace picks up. Our skin flushes and our eyes open wider. Our bodies also tell us when we aren't close to our Driving Passion: We don't have visceral reactions to things that do not matter to us. No matter how much we may say something matters, we cannot fool our skin—our stomach—our hearts and our lungs. But when we feel that quickening, that excitement—when we want to pump our fist like an athlete who has just scored the winning point—that's the body telling us that Driving Passion is engaged.

Think about it for a minute. When do you feel most physically alive? When are you tempted to run a 5K or chop wood in your backyard or run around the block or wrestle with your kids? It is most likely when you are thinking about or doing the thing that is your Driving Passion.

Indicator Number Three is *Psychological Well-Being.*

At present the American Well-Being Index is 66%, at least according to the Gallup-Healthways Well-Being Index. And that's a good thing—but not great.

How do you measure well-being? To do so, the Gallup organization, which, along with Healthways, initiated the Gallup-Healthways Well-Being Index (WBI) in 2008. They began by interviewing at least 500 U.S. adults every day which resulted in real-time measurement and insights on how respondents feel about their life and overall outlook, physical health, emotional health, healthy behavior, work environment and quality, and basic access to health and life resources. In short, a Well-Being Index.

So what is your well-being index at today? On a scale where 100% is perfect, how do you feel right now about your life? If you are engaged with activity or work that taps into your Driving Passion, chances are you are scoring pretty high. The fact is when you are doing the thing you are meant to do, the thing that ignites your passion, your well-being increases. You feel good about yourself, and you feel positively about your life. You may have problems, but those problems do not debilitate you. You may experience sadness, but that sadness does not cripple you. It does not take you out of the game. You are OK. You are moving forward.

Why is this? Because you have found something that nurtures your soul, that excites your brain, and enlivens your heart. You have found your Driving Passion.

We are passionate about helping you discover your Driving Passion!

So remember, your Driving Passion is the "fuel" or energizing force that drives your outcomes.

No matter what "context" you enter into—work, home, hobby, family—your Driving Passion energizing attribute is consistent.

Remember George, our cello player? He says, "I start on a piece of music on a new instrument and I can't rest until I have mastered the notes. His driving passion is not the mastering of a new instrument or learning more music...it is his burning desire to overcome obstacles. In a different context, George's burning desire to overcome obstacles is also what motivated him to get an unrestricted driver's license. (George drives with his feet).

Your Driving Passion is a compelling yearning—an intense appetite. Jeff, our entrepreneur from Chapter 2, says, "I get an idea and the questions start to flow and I can not stop until I have answers as to how to move forward with a plan." Jeff is energized as he develops creative solutions. His intense appetite for answers illustrates his Driving Passion. Ángel's intense appetite was to improve with every new attempt at the task set before him.

Driving Passion requires we do something—it demands action. Driving Passion is often difficult to articulate because it is internal: "inside" of you, intangible, and non-transitory. However, where words may fail you, your actions speak loud and clear. People know by your actions what you are passionate about. Remember the cab driver, now my friend, Lucio? His action convinces me I am safe with him in a city that has not always been known to be safe.

Driving Passion is emotional, it is highly personal, and it is often such an automatic energizer for each of us that we do not realize it is at work every day. You can't not have a Driving Passion. You may not know how to label it, you might be ignoring it, you can suppress it, you can deny it, but your Driving Passion is in existence right now inside of you.

Your life is a story with distinct chapters illustrating your Driving Passion. You have something deep inside of you that wants to address a need and contribute to the world, and this is all about your Driving Passion. The people who know you best see that something in you calling out to something bigger and greater and this is all about your Driving Passion.

Are you beginning to see it?

The fastest way to determine your Driving Passion is to go back to Chapter 3 and revisit the exercise you did on your Critical Outcome. Then you can choose to do the exercise below now, or read onto the next chapter and come back later.

Application: Understanding Your Driving Passion.

Start by asking yourself these questions:

What keeps me up at night?

What do I think about over and over again?

What ignites my creativity?

These are the questions that you have to ask yourself to unlock your Driving Passion (DP). Again, go with your gut. Don't respond with an answer that you feel is "correct," but don't really believe. Don't try to second-guess what you *should* answer. Don't feel that you have to have the perfect answer. You're not competing for the Miss America crown or participating in a presidential debate. This is a highly personal exercise, but a vital one. The only right answers are the honest ones. We are trying to find out what drives you to take action?

Maybe your answer is "clean water" or "love" or "an end to war" or "faith." Maybe it's something that you fear sounds trivial, like "getting just the right sound from my instrument" or "making that one piece of wood perfectly smooth." It could be anything. The only thing that matters is that your answer is true to you and resonates with your heart.

Your next assignment is to stop whatever you are doing (We're serious about "right now"—this is the sort of thing that is easy to forget to do if you don't engage it in the moment) and text or call several people who know you really well and ask them this question: "What do you think is the one thing that motivates me? What do you think is the one thing I am the most passionate about?"

Record those answers below:

Now we want to challenge you further with these questions:

First question, "What keeps you from following the passion that is in your heart?"

Make a list of the impediments or obstacles to you following your passion:

What would you do if the items on the list above did not stand in your way?

Next question, "If you had all of the money and time in the world, what would you do?"

What would you do to impact the world? Make a list starting with the most urgent need you would satisfy.

Here is where it all comes together.

1. What do you believe to be the world's greatest need.
2. What do others say is the "one thing" for you.
3. If you had unlimited time and money, what would you do.

Put all of these together and you will have a glimpse of your Driving Passion.

Here's the key message to you about your Driving Passion from the questions above:

1. Asking yourself what you believe to be the world's biggest need, illustrates what your values are—what drives you.
2. And what your friends believe to be true about you reveals the one thing that drives you.
3. Fantasizing about what you would do if you had unlimited time and money lets you imagine life without barriers, and allows you to more fully imagine the possibilities of following your Driving Passion.

If you dare, in the space below write out what you believe to be your Driving Passion. Go ahead. Be bold. Be honest.

Notes:

CHAPTER FIVE

What's Your ID:

YOUR ASSIMILATED EXPERIENCE?

The other day, we had an appointment with the subject of our next interview in Southern California. We started our day as normal, with no word from her. Then, at 10:30 sharp she walked in. She was right on time for our meeting, but to our surprise her arm was in a sling, and she was walking with a slight limp in her step.

We were understandably concerned. When we asked she told us how she had been side swiped by a distracted California driver the evening before while cycling. We told her we would have re-scheduled had we known of her accident.

She would not hear of it. "This meeting is important and I meant to keep it," she told us.

We sensed right away that Selwa Al-Hazzaa—wife, mother and physician was willing to share her life *and* her Assimilated Experience with us.

Dr. Selwa Al-Hazzaa (Arabic: سلوى الهزاع) is the head of the ophthalmology department at King Faisal Specialist Hospital. She is one of the most influential people in Saudi Arabia, and the Arab world in general. She is one of the very first Saudi women to achieve international success in both the academic and professional arenas.

At a young age Selwa moved with her family from Riyadh, Saudi Arabia, to Tucson, Arizona. She studied at Tucson High School, and then moved back with her family to Riyadh, Saudi Arabia to complete high school.

Despite considerable social pressure not to pursue her education, Selwa persisted. With her family's support and encouragement she enrolled at King Saud University to study medicine. She married a fellow Saudi and moved with him to Washington, DC, where he worked at the Royal Embassy of Saudi Arabia. Despite this dislocation, she continued to pursue her studies—transferring to Johns Hopkins University.

After that, she moved back to Riyadh to work at King Faisal Specialist Hospital. She published many papers, including one featuring innovative research about genetically inherited eye diseases in Saudi Arabia. In 1997, she became the first female department head in the history of King Faisal Specialist Hospital.

In that same year she appeared in Marquis *Who's Who in the World* Publication Board's fourteenth edition as one of the most prominent personalities for that year. A year after that, in 1998, she was chosen as woman of the year by the American Biographical Institute.

Dr. Al Hazzaa credits her father and her husband for helping her become the person she is today. But it was a different relative whom she credits with igniting within her the driving passion that fuels her leadership and work. She told us this story:

"We were attending a family gathering, and I was standing a little distance from my father not visible by the persons talking with him. I was within earshot when I heard my uncle saying to my father, 'What a huge difference Selwa and your other four daughters could make in our country if only they were boys.'"

That's when it had struck her: how often she had been the only girl in her class. How often she heard her girlhood friends talk about giving up their studies, leaving school, or abandoning career dreams for the more traditional roles of homemaker or stay-at-home mother. In Selwa's family, it was normal for her and her sisters to go to school—and college and then graduate school. It was normal for them to have dreams beyond the family. Until that moment, she hadn't realized how unusual such horizons were in a country where traditional gender roles are still the norm.

"I never forgot that experience," she says now, remembering that one overheard comment. "It has inspired and convinced me. It gave me the conviction to shape a new reality for all Saudi women." That's how Assimilated Experience works, _it's an historical perspective, an event or incident from the past that shapes, informs and directs our behavior in the present_.

She recalls, "That experience for some reason always comes to mind when I am asked what motivates me. It is clear it made an indelible impression upon me. Since that moment I've just always seen myself as making things better for my kids and the next generation. Not better in that I think we had it bad, but better in that they can shape our country to exude it's strength and poise."

In Saudi Arabia, female doctors care for only female patients. With the rarest of exceptions, they do not provide medical care for men. It just does not happen.

Yet Dr. Al Hazzaa became the personal ophthalmologist to the late King Fahad.

Inconceivable.

As we interviewed her, it was clear that she is aware of her difference. "I am the exception. I am the type of person that regardless of the limitations put on me, I don't put limitations on myself. I shatter those limitations. In fact, I try to outdo myself after every achievement," she said.

As we write this, Dr. Al-Hazzaa is still blazing new trails. As per Royal Decree from King Abdullah, Dr. Al-Hazzaa she became one of the first ever female members of the Saudi Arabia Shoura Council. This is the council that formulates recommendations to the King!

In response to this latest honor she says, "But there are a lot of women like me. And it's us, the women who are the exception, who make the difference for those who can not, or do not have a voice." Women in Saudi Arabia form only 4% of the workforce.

Selwa's unique, predictable and notably excellent results are demonstrated in the intentional way she respects and honors Arab custom and history, even as she serves as a trailblazer, a female leader in a very traditional world. That is what she is known for in the Arab world—a woman who is a powerful global leader and yet maintains respectful in adherence to Arab faith and culture. This is her Critical Outcome. Her Driving Passion is to create a platform for other Arab women—to be a role model for Arab women who like her respect their heritage and yet have significant leadership contributions to make. So the ID dimensions connect like this, Critical Outcome is fueled by Driving Passion and Driving Passion is initiated by Assimilated Experience. We will return to this later, in greater detail.

The comment Selwa overheard about her and her four sisters, ignited a compelling yearning within her to show that Arab women can and should be leaders! This is what drives her, what gets her up in the morning and what energizes her as she travels the world speaking on Faith, Work and Women in leadership.

Our experiences go a long way to shape who we are as adults.

If we grew up with a secure home life full of love and respect and affirmation, it makes sense on an intuitive level that we will be more likely to experience the world as a safe and positive place.

If we lost a parent at an early age, it seems likely the opposite will be true: that we will be more likely to believe life is uncertain and the other shoe might be just about to drop.

If we experienced athletic success, we are likely to be confident. If we were shunned as a child, it would seem natural we would be more likely to be suspicious of new relationships.

Our experiences have a profound ability to shape our lives, for good or for ill.

But it's worth reminding ourselves some people have really difficult life experiences and yet grow up to be caring and resourceful people. Others grow up breezing through life yet later have difficulty finding their place in the world. What's the difference? Why does one child from a happy background grow up unfulfilled and unable to contribute, while another—from a hard-luck life—becomes a leader and a significant contributor?

Because it is not the life experiences that shape us. It is in the way we *assimilate* our life experiences that makes us who we are. Take this story from the late Fred Rogers, famed broadcaster and host of the television series, *Mr. Rogers Neighborhood*:

"A few years ago, I was asked to be part of a White House meeting about children and television. Many broadcasters from all over the country were there. Since I was supposed to be one of the speakers, I was seated beside Mrs. Clinton, who afterward said, "Congratulations," as she was whisked away to her next meeting. But as I was leaving that enormous room, I heard something from one of the military guards, who was all dressed up in white and gold looking like a statue. I heard him whisper, "'Thanks, Mr. Rogers.'"

So I went over to him, noticed that his eyes were moist, and I asked him, "Thanks for what?"

"'Well, sir,'" he said, "'as I listened to you today, I started to remember my grandfather's brother. I haven't thought about him in years. I was only seven when he died, but just before that, he gave me his favorite fishing rod. I've just been thinking, maybe that's why I like fishing so much and why I like to show the kids in my neighborhood all about it.'"

'That was it. As far as I'm concerned, the major reason for my going to Washington that day was that military guard and nourishing the memory of his great-uncle. What marvelous mysteries we're privileged to be part of! Why would that young man be assigned to guard that particular room on that particular day? It's slender threads like that that weave the complex fabric of our life together."

Fred Rogers, captures in his last sentence above, what we believe about Assimilated Experience—your experiences, when assimilated, 'weave the fabric of your life together,' into a unique tapestry—they make you, you. What is the moment or moments that have shaped you? What specific incident, day or instance comes to mind? Remember Selwa and that overheard conversation? Like her, and the Marine above, some of us do have profound and life-altering single experiences, however, most of us are shaped by the collection of experiences we go through—a combination of good and bad, painful and wonderful.

We may not have any choice about where we were born—or to whom—but, as adults, we do have choice in how we use that experience. How we assimilate it. The question for us in this chapter is whether or not we will be intentional about understanding and thinking about and acting on our assimilated life experience.

So, how does our Assimilated Experience play out in our lives? We see three primary ways.

First our Assimilated Experience *impacts our natural self.*

Remember our byword—you are so you!

You are born with much of who you are—your temperament and wiring and proclivities.

But, as many have pointed out, not only nature but also nurture shapes who you are. Your experiences make a big difference to the person you are becoming.

Notice we didn't simply say your Assimilated Experience impacts your self. We added the word "natural" very intentionally. Who you are inherently is very important. But it is not all-determinative. Remember, different people respond to similar life experiences in profoundly unique ways. The combination of your natural self and your individual experiences is unique to you.

Assimilated Experience also *gives us perspective.*

What is perspective, exactly? It's how you see a thing, a person, an experience, or a question. Your angle, your "take" on life. And how you see that thing depends on where you are standing and what experiences you bring to the table.

There is a very famous painting in St. Petersburg, Russia, depicting the biblical narrative of the return of the Prodigal Son. The story of the Prodigal Son is one of forgiveness, a metaphor for all the embracing love of the Divine. But it is made more dramatic, and more powerful, by putting it in human terms. The prodigal son is, literally, the bad boy. The son who didn't do what he was supposed to, who squandered his gifts. He wastes his time and his resources, and he rejects his family. But then, lost, lonely, hungry, and tired, he comes home. And that is the moment captured by this painting.

In that culture, in that time, such a son—broke, sick, hungry—would not expect a hearty welcome. He would expect to be punished, even shunned, by his family. After all, *he* had rejected *them* first.

But that's not what we see in this painting. What we see is the moment the prodigal child appears. And at the center of the painting is the father who surprises his wayward son by rushing to embrace him. A father, who would be expected to disown a disrespectful son, or worse, instead runs forward to take him in his arms.

It is a dramatic moment by any light. But there's another drama going on among the viewers. That's the drama of perspective. Of, if you will, point of view. Curators say patrons of the museum come to that painting and they split into one of two camps. Curators say some patrons fix their gaze on the father in the painting, expressing admiration for his strength and compassion. Others are focused on the startled and grateful son.

Why do you think that is? Don't you guess that it has an awful lot to do with the perspective each viewer of the painting brings to his or her viewing?

Let's say you are a parent who has a once-wayward child, who has been reconciled to you. The painting might well call up feelings of happiness and gratitude. But supposed your wayward child is still estranged from you. You might feel sadness or a sense of loss. What if you were the wayward child? What if you feel you squandered gifts your family tried to give you, and now, as an adult, you are aware of what you lost—of the way you hurt your family? You might look at this reunion and feel joy for the son who was able to admit his mistakes. Or might you look at the father and feel sadness at your own lost chances? And if you were lucky enough to have reconciliation like this one, might you not look at the surprise and the joy on the son's face and remember your own blessings? Your own second chances—and feel compelled to offer such chances to others?

The painting is the same but the response to viewing it is radically different. That is because our perspective is shaped by our Assimilated Experience.

You see how this truth informs every area of our lives, from our workplace interactions, to our family relationships, to the way we feel about hot-button political issues? Our perspective can—and will—

change over time. And as it changes, it alters how we view our lives, how we assimilate our experience.

Our friend Jeff Hussey from an earlier chapter says that he has "pattern recognition" when it comes to certain issues. When it comes to areas of risk and employee selection and investments he has an intuitive sense of how much to put on the table, whom to hire, and where to place his and his clients' hard-earned money. Where do you think that comes from? Some of it is Jeff's natural self, to be sure—he was making money as an entrepreneur as a pre-teen, if you will recall. But over time, as he has lost a job, experienced bankruptcy, lost some money on real estate development, and built a phenomenally successful technology company, his perspective has been altered dramatically.

Here's the exciting thing—YOU have pattern recognition as well. It might not be in business. It might be in human relationships, or athletic endeavors, or in the arena of where to invest your time and energy. It's worth thinking about this. Where has your Assimilated Experience helped to shape you in such a way that you see things others don't? You recognize patterns and come to conclusions faster than others do. Because of this, you can almost anticipate what will happen next—and seemingly make the right decisions on a regular basis. Do you see how your Assimilated Experience has shaped your perspective in such a way that you are a step ahead?

Our Assimilated Experience also *shapes who we are becoming.*

One of the most important and encouraging truths we want you to bring from your investment in reading our book is the knowledge that you are not a finished product. Yes, you have a lifetime's worth of habits and experiences, triumphs and failures, broken hearts and passionate romances. But you are not done with you yet!

Meet Brad, a very successful medical devices sales executive. Brad puts a high premium on his reputation for integrity. He says, "Before I can sell the least expensive medical screw, or the largest, most expensive diagnostic machine, I have to be successful in selling myself, people have to know that I can be trusted." So when we asked him to relate an incident or moment that has shaped his life, he chose one that had to do with his integrity been questioned. Brad told us how many years ago he was dealing with a major customer who accused him of lacking integrity. The customer—and we mean a **major** customer—went so far as to call Brad's boss in another country and tell him "If you keep this man in your organization then you lack integrity too!" Brad was shell-shocked and taken aback. He had not been at fault.

"It did not matter how big a customer this guy was and how much was at stake for me, I decided then and there that I could not work with him anymore or work with anyone like him."

"That is," Brad said, "until months later, when I came to own my part in the perception the client had of me."

Brad told us how he came to understand the situation differently: "I was involved with putting together a sale with this particular client who accused me of a lack of integrity. But, I was also at the same time selling the same idea to other clients, which is normal and accepted practice. Everyone in our industry knows that because of the pace and need for new products being brought to market, we usually pitch the idea simultaneously to several prospective buyers. I found out later that this client felt that he had exclusive options on the idea we were selling. So, when he came back to me (weeks after our initial conversation) to say he was ready to move forward, I had to tell him he was too late as another client had already signed and executed a contract. It was not that he could not have the product but it was that he was not going to be the first to have it. He was angry about that and accused me of lying, of collusion and of lacking integrity. I was angry too and it took me months before I was able to see his side of the story. Now, I put in writing that we present our product ideas to a select number of clients simultaneously and not to just one party. I state very clearly up front that it is to the client who makes an acceptable offer first to whom we will sell our idea first. That experience influenced how I approach not only my process for selling ideas, but more so how I can choose to be more objective when my integrity is challenged."

This painful professional event for Brad probably reminds you of one or more of your *own* similar experience. But like him, we benefit every time we take note of how our Assimilated Experience informs, shapes and directs our behavior.

Remember, you were made different to make a difference—never forget that. You are still in the process of becoming—becoming great, we believe. Your Assimilated Experience has had a profound influence on you, but you are not limited by your failures and hurts nor predestined to greatness by your triumphs and successes. It's all about what you do with these experiences, and we want to help you think through how to be intentional about that.

So, we are going to ask you to do something you have probably done before, but in a way you have probably never done it!

We're going to ask you to write a Resumé—two Resumés, actually. The first one may be tough to write. Just as likely, it will be insight-producing and cathartic. We'd like you to write a Resumé of your failures. That's right—a Failure Resumé.

No, we're not asking you to inflict undue pain on yourself. This is going somewhere good. Simply make a bullet point lists of the most significant failures of your life—personally and professionally. Don't analyze them right now, or try to make sense of them, or figure out (yet) what you learned from them. Just list them:

My Failure Resumé
-
-
-

-
-

Any surprises?

OK, now your task gets more fun. We know that you have enjoyed great successes in your personal or professional life—marrying the girl of your dreams, raising a great kid, leading the company in sales five straight years, seeing your direct reports go on to increased management responsibility of their own, watching seven of your once-Cub Scouts go on to serve their community as Eagle Scouts.

So, write out your personal Success Resumé. Define success how you want, but please be generous to yourself. Again, this is not about analysis at the moment, but about listing bullet points:

My Success Resumé
-
-
-
-
-

Now, let's put those resumés together. Take time—make sure you allow some focused time for this—and see where there are correlations between your Success Resumé and your Failure Resumé.

For example, maybe you disappointed a teacher. Think back on that teacher, a special educator who had invested in you. But you failed that teacher—maybe you even failed the class—and you felt bad, like you had let that special teacher down. That special teacher saw you fail. But what that teacher did not know was that you were struggling with an undiagnosed learning disability. Now, you are a classroom volunteer who has unusual success encouraging and mentoring underperforming students. Do you see how both of those instances of your Assimilated Experience have shaped who you are and have altered your perspective?

There is real magic in seeing these correlations between instances of success and failure in our lives. They are not random or arbitrary. We believe that the universe is much more purposeful than that and that beginning to make sense of your Assimilated Experience will bring real insight into things in your lives you have not previously connected and will help unlock your Intentional Difference.

What you are doing here is actually assimilating your life experiences, seeing your life more as an ongoing story than a series of unconnected events. You are not the sole author of your story, but you play a huge part and one of the most effective ways to shape and tell your own life story is by pulling the threads from your Assimilated Experience together.

You can use the space below to make a list of the correlations and connections between items on your Success and Failure Resumés. Have fun!

CHAPTER SIX

What's Your ID:

YOUR CUMULATIVE KNOWLEDGE?

"My wife Julann just came up with the idea one day when we were in a plane bringing us back to New York from Duluth," said Merv Griffin, explaining the origins of the game show "Jeopardy."

"I was mulling over game show ideas, when she noted that there had not been a successful question-and-answer game on the air since the quiz show scandals. Why not do a switch, she suggested, and give the answers to the contestant and let them come up with the question? She fired a couple of answers to me: '5,280'—and the question of course was 'How many feet in a mile?' Another was '79 Wistful Vista'; that was Fibber and Mollie McGee's address. I loved the idea, went straight to NBC with the idea, and they bought it without even looking at a pilot show," said

Griffin, explaining the origin of the show, which tests contestants on how well they can tap into the knowledge they have amassed over time.

Of course the network loved it. They knew—as we all do—that we are constantly acquiring just the kind of knowledge that would make the show work.

You know things. Whoever you are, wherever you are from, you have stuff that you know.

This stuff that you know, we call it Cumulative Knowledge, is an accumulated body of knowledge that is unique to us. We gather and retain it over time. Naturally. Easily. It sticks to us. We learn it quickly without effort. It is accessible to us, and we regularly put it to productive use.

You may not know how to program code or hot-wire an engine, or change out an HVAC system or throw the perfect spiral (or maybe you do!) but there are things that you *know*.

Probably not too many things, but there are a few. Whether you are gregarious or easy-going, there is knowledge that you have acquired effortlessly over time… Stuff that you *know*, deep down in the bedrock of your soul.

Those things form our Cumulative Knowledge.

Here is how we define the dimension of Cumulative Knowledge:

Cumulative Knowledge is the *unique retention and purposeful, productive use of information*.

Let's break that down.

Cumulative Knowledge is the *unique* retention of information. Without having to work at it, there is certain type of information each of us retain easily. For some it is verbal, such as the punch line to a joke. For others, it is auditory, such as persons with the ability to identify a note with perfect pitch—piano tuners for example—they are able to retain the distinct sound of a single musical note. Still for others like expert sales people, it is the array of facial expressions, the subtle body language and word choices that they have come to recognize as buying signals. Cumulative Knowledge is what you learn easily and are able to put to purposeful and productive use. It's that which is sticky to you. Its like we have our own built in information sorter or filter. Some information just rushes right by us without sticking or being noticed. Other information, we latch onto: we value it, we own it, and we never let it go. It becomes ours to use and apply and morph with other incoming sticky information.

Here's another way of thinking about it.

If you and a group of friends were given three pages of a book and asked to underline what you believed to be the most pertinent insights, chances are you would underline slightly (or maybe extremely) different words. This is because the knowledge that strikes you as most fascinating or relevant is drawn from your unique experience. Remember what we learned in the last chapter? We learned that each of us experience unique historical mile-marker events that we assimilate. Some of us have singular events, like Selwa overhearing that particular conversation. Others have multiple incidents like Jeff Hussey selling soap as a kid to his neighbors, then as an adult, getting fired for hacking into the computer at work in order to reach more clients. These type events make up our Assimilated Experience—the historical perspective that informs, shapes and directs our behavior. What we are about to learn, is how our Assimilated Experience, is informed by our Cumulative Knowledge. At this point we see the interaction of the ID dimensions like this— our Critical Outcome is fueled by our Driving Passion; our Driving Passion is initiated by our Assimilated Experience; and our Assimilated Experience is informed by our Cumulative Knowledge. How you assimilate experience is unique to you, in the same way, what type of knowledge you retain, how you acquire knowledge and how you apply that knowledge is also unique to you.

Cumulative Knowledge is the unique *retention* of information. You can't forget the lessons you have learned, They are stored in your mental filing cabinet—your brain—coded in a way that makes it easy for you to recall when needed:

You were in elementary school and you were called upon to make a presentation. You had forgotten (alas!) to prepare but nevertheless you were on stage in front of thirty other kids and an eager teacher. Your presentation was supposed to be on the Declaration of Independence. You knew nothing about the Declaration of Independence.

But the night before your dad, a Civil War buff, had gathered the kids in the living room and read aloud President Lincoln's Gettysburg Address. He had savored the words and explained the context. You loved it.

So, the next day you are in your classroom, all eyes on you, expected to wax eloquent about the Founding Fathers, and you have nothing.

So, out of nowhere, you paint the picture of the Gettysburg battlefield and the reedy-voiced President with the stovetop hat and the words that ring down through history.

At the end, your classmates and your teacher burst out into applause, even though you have totally muffed the assignment. And you have learned something:

I have the ability to grasp history, paint a picture, and think on my feet.
Or this.

You are hoping for an internship with a motor racing team after your second year in college. Your dreams are of NASCAR or Formula 1. But that falls through and you end up working in your dad's best friend's real estate office, doing menial labor. But as a result of that summer you understand—for the rest of your life—the way the housing market works and the emotions prospective buyers and sellers go through, and you learn how to calibrate a sale. You would not have known these things unless you had been in that office that summer in that setting in that market. And you have learned something:

I know how people think and react and what they dream of when they are contemplating making one of the biggest purchases of their lives.

These are life lessons that cannot be taken away from you, ever, and they form a base of knowledge affecting how you live life every single day.

But in order for our Cumulative Knowledge to be effective in our lives we have to determine to *purposefully* use it every single day.

Abu Bakr put it this way: "Without knowledge, action is useless, and knowledge without action is futile."

Do you see the linkage between Assimilated Experience and Cumulative Knowledge (remember that each of the six dimensions are linked one with another)?

It is the Experience that shapes us. And it is the Knowledge that we pull from having gone through the Experience that informs how our lives actually become more purposeful and intentional. This changes how we think, feel, and act in all of our decisions and relationships.

So, exactly how do we learn how to think, feel, and act? In two ways.

First, we learn by *doing*. We build our knowledge by assessing and evaluating how certain actions and behaviors we practice are responded to by others. We learn what "works" and what doesn't work in certain situations.

As you learn more about your ID, you begin to see in what proportion each of your six dimensions are best applied given a particular circumstance.

You examine and are in tune with the cues and clues given off by others to the ways you interact, the things you say, the actions you take.

Your brain is amazing! It is amazingly capable of addressing a remarkably diverse range of situations, rapidly processing the experiences you have had and applying the knowledge you have gleaned from those experiences.

You also learn by *not doing*.

Think back to when you were a kid. You see another kid who is reprimanded and punished for a specific action. What do you do? Your amazing brain builds that knowledge into your own internal database as something you shouldn't do (I won't throw spitballs at the teacher because I saw what happened to Jim and I know that the same thing would happen to me!). So, you are accumulating knowledge that is secondhand and external to you as well as firsthand and internal.

In a way, your brain works in the same way that a computer utilizes "cookies," the digital place-markers that track your online interactions and Internet surfing. The cookies note recurring patterns and experiences you have online and serve to help marketing companies predict what you are interested in reading about, purchasing, and receiving more of. It's all about accumulating data and applying that data to the fabric of your everyday life.

Your Greatest Teacher

Take a moment and consider an important question: Who was the greatest teacher you have ever had in your life? This person could be a classroom teacher, a coach, a mentor, a relative… it doesn't matter. What matters is that she or he stood out from the crowd as a uniquely great and influential teacher for you. Write that person's name below:

Now, consider this second question and write your reflections in the blank space:

What knowledge deposits did this great teacher make in my life?

A third question—What other knowledge investments have you received in your life? (These might be diplomas, degrees, continuing education classes, on-the-job training, books, video curriculum, you name it…) Write the most important ones below:

Now, a very purposeful question: How are you specifically applying those knowledge deposits to your day-to-day life, right now? Of all of the things your great teacher taught you, which are the ones that still show up today? Out of all the classes you have taken, educational opportunities you have taken advantage of, online courses you have worked through, books you have read, what are the nuggets of information that still impact the way you think speak and act? We invite you to make a list below:

Finally, a very important question as we turn from history to the present. Look at the various areas of your life, relationships, work, service to others, etc. do you see some ways you can more intentionally put to use what it is you learn easily?

CHAPTER SEVEN

What's Your ID:

YOUR EMERGENT SKILL?

There is something—maybe a few 'somethings'—that you have always been able to do well.

Probably your parents or a teacher pointed it out to you when you were quite young.

You could fix things easily, things that others assumed were irretrievably broken. Or you could do figures in your head without having to count on your fingers or use a calculator. Perhaps you could run faster and farther than others or draw more beautiful pictures. Maybe you noticed things others didn't or had a memory others described as photographic.

Whatever IT was, it was so *you*!

This thing came naturally to you, and it was not a one-time or even occasional occurrence. It happened all the time, repeating itself in predictable patterns. You came to count on yourself for this thing, and others learned to count on you for it.

This thing is your *Emergent Skill*. It's the thing that has always come naturally to you. Chances are it may come so natural to you that you're not totally cognizant of it. Maybe others have noticed and pointed it out to you or you have come to realize it yourself because it's slightly different than other people.

Here's how we define Emergent Skill: it is the *innate ability that finds automatic and repeated expression*.

As the legendary jazz musician Charlie Parker said, "If it's not in you, it won't come out of your horn." All along, you have been playing a song that is unique to you—all of your life utilizing your Emergent Skill. Now you get the chance to be even more intentional about it, about this powerful part of who you are.

Your Emergent Skill is an *innate ability*.

For your whole life there has been at least a trace of this skill. Even if you have not had the opportunity, time or inclination to refine or master your skill, it has been there. Whether it is musical talent, athletic prowess, organizational ability, connecting others to opportunities or relationships, critical thinking or acute powers of observation, it's there.

No matter what obstacles might have gotten in the way of your skill, nothing can prevent it from emerging. It gushes out of you.

One of our clients, Misse, has organizational ability gushing out of her. Standing just five feet two inches tall, with a petite body frame, Misse brings undeniably unique value in her role as administrative assistant. "I love to bring order out of chaos!," she says, with her usual exuberance. But this skill did not emerge under the tutelage of a mentor or while she was taking a project management course.

You see, when Misse was only a toddler her parents would observe her removing the family's canned goods from the lazy susan under their kitchen counter. She would spread the cans on the floor, organize them by the color of their labels, and then meticulously place them back in their correct places. Do you see what this means? At two years old, Misse already had her own information sorter and filter. She was already demonstrating her unique retention and purposeful use of information—her Cumulative Knowledge. But what caught her parents' attention was the automatic expression of her innate ability to organize, to impose structure! Two years old: unable to read, but she had pattern recognition—enough to know that she preferred sameness and order. She saw how things were *supposed* to go, and she knew that she was the one to make that happen.

Here again, lets look at the connection between the ID dimensions: our Critical Outcome is fueled by our Driving Passion; our Driving Passion is initiated by our Assimilated Experience; our Assimilated Experience is informed by our Cumulative Knowledge; and our Cumulative Knowledge is expressed by our Emergent Skill.

Your special skill, like Misse's, has always been there—it is part of the very fabric of who you are. It is part of what makes you uniquely you.

Now, you might be able to live with corn kernels next to green beans or sweet potatoes side by side with asparagus spears…but not Misse! No, her emergent skill of organization and administration was evident in her even when she was only two years old.

Your Emergent Skill is like that for you. It is innate—you did not have to seek it out. And it is an ability—it cannot be denied. It must be expressed!

Oh, that word "expressed" is really important. A true Emergent Skill is not something we wish we had or hope to have one day. It just happens automatically for you and it is undeniable to you and to those who know you best. It repeats itself again and again in whatever arena of life you are engaging at the moment.

It is automatic and repeated. If you have a job that direct deposits your paycheck to your bank account, you know what we mean. Every fifteen or thirty days your bank balance increases by the same amount. You don't even have to think about it. And it happens every time (well, we hope so!).

You become delightfully predictable in your productivity and in the results you get. And people notice!

If you are an administrative assistant, like Misse, you will be called upon for organizational tasks at work, to be sure. But you'll also be asked to administrate the canned goods drive at your kids' school, the offering collection procedure at your church, and the neighborhood progressive dinner at Christmas time!

Now, let's be clear—when it comes to your Emergent Skill you have not yet arrived. And it is at this moment we can talk about becoming intentional around your skills. See, this is when your Emergent Skill moves from this thing that has just always been there to this unstoppable force that can take you to productive heights you never dreamed of scaling and enhance the lives of those around you.

Your Emergent Skill becomes more powerful with time and productively applied energy. In fact, as you become more proficient, your Emergent Skill becomes even more natural. It will take less time and energy for you to accomplish great results as you develop your Emergent Skill. As a matter of fact, you will find you are receiving energy rather than depleting it. You may even lose track of time while engaged in that emergent skill.

Your capacity for accuracy and proficiency becomes much greater the more you work on your Emergent Skill.

Now, we don't want to oversell. You won't get better each and every time you use intentionally your Emergent Skill. If you are a runner, for example, you won't set a personal record each and every time you run a 5K race.

But over time, with great intentionality, you will see real, lasting results in terms of productivity, effectiveness, and even personal joy!

What might that look like?

Perhaps you have heard of the writer Malcolm Gladwell's concept of mastery. The idea is that if you repeat an activity for 10,000 hours the activity will be so ingrained in your muscle memory and/or your rehearsed mental and intellectual habits that the activity will flow from you. You will be able to do it seemingly automatically, without thinking or making conscious choices. The ability will simply be there for you—as automatic as breathing.

According to Gladwell, you could be in the very top percentile of people in the world doing that thing.

Gladwell suggests you almost won't even have to think about what you are doing. And others will be very quick to see that you are becoming exceptional in your mastery. That will be because you have expended a tremendous amount of time, energy, and repeated application on that particular skill.

So, how do we marry the 10,000 hours to mastery concept to Emergent Skill?

We'll use two analogies—one for sports fans and one for music fans.

Picture Tiger Woods. By all accounts, one of the most physically gifted golfers in history and also one of the most dogged practicers of all time. He spent well over 10,000 hours hitting balls, honing his short game, and putting the ball on greens of all configurations until the results were center cut.

Yo-Yo Ma is considered to be the greatest cellist of all time, recognized from the time he was a small child as an once-in-a-lifetime talent. And, like Woods, he is famous for his maniacal devotion to his craft.

Now, let's say you decided you wanted to be a golfer. Or a cellist. A really great golfer and an unusually skilled cellist.

You've read our book and you buy Malcolm's idea of 10,000 hours to mastery.

So you hire a top golf pro and spend 10,000 hours on the practice range, the putting green and on the course honing your craft. You find a music professor at the finest conservatory and devote your 10,000 hours to practicing the cello.

What's going to happen at the end of that time? Well, you *may* be an exceptional golfer. And you *may* be one heck of a cellist. Or *NOT*!

Why not?

Because for Woods and Ma, playing golf and the cello are part of their Emergent Skill. More likely than not, they are not part of yours (but, if they are, by all means get to work logging your 10,000 hours!). Remember our definition of Emergent Skill? It is, an innate ability that finds automatic and repeated expression. It gushes out, has to find a way out, like water forcing its way out through the slightest opening.

One of our interviewees told us about the love for music he had passed on to his small son. Note that we say his *love* for music. Not brilliance or talent. Our friend is brilliant in many walks of life, but he doesn't have any particular musical skill. He just enjoys messing around with his guitar.

But his son does have real musical skill, a talent that has been evident from the first time he picked up an instrument at age seven. His instrument of choice is the viola, and in his hands that instrument— deeper-voiced than the violin—sings. As our friend said to us, "Something very different happens when my son picks up the viola than what happens when I pick up the guitar." Our friend plays around for fun. His son, on the other hand, makes music—and always has.

Do you see it? Your Emergent Skill just gushes out of you. You notice it and others notice it about you early on in life. This remarkable ability emerges prior to you receiving any formal training—and still you get better at doing it with each use!

So the key in optimizing this dimension of your Intentional Difference is to determine what your unique, once-in-a-lifetime, individual, 'gushing out of *you*" Emergent Skill is or are.

The rest of this chapter contains exercises designed to help you make this life-changing discovery.

And before we get started, keep this in mind. Being a master at your Emergent Skill, according to Malcolm Gladwell's research, will take a 10,000-hour commitment. If you are just getting started, the master who is you may be 10 years in the future. It will take big-time devotion and practice. But it will all be worth it when you are a Master!

Personal Exercise

1. Think back to when you were twelve years old or younger. What did you do exceptionally well?

2. People noticed me doing_____ well at an early age.

3. When you were in high school, how would you fill in the blank when people said to you, "You know, you are really talented at _____"?

4. As you grew up with that innate skill, in what activities was it demonstrated? _____

5. Is it a major part of your life and work today? How? _____
    _____

6. What are some next steps you can take to grow these innate abilities into amazing skills?

    Step 1 _____

    Step 2 _____

    Step 3 _____

7. Are there some things you are doing in your life right now that you should stop doing so that you will have the bandwidth, time, and energy to invest into your innate skills?

    Stop doing_____

    Stop doing_____

    Stop doing_____

8. What are two areas of your Emergent Skill dimension where you can commit to making the investment to gain mastery?

    To gain mastery I must invest in _____

    To gain mastery I must invest in _____

9. In the space below, write some personal statements of declaration promising yourself that you will begin that journey.

10. I_____(your name in the blank) do declare that I will devote_____(minutes, hours, days) doing_____in order to increase mastery of my_____(skill).

CHAPTER EIGHT

What's Your ID:

YOUR PREVAILING TALENT?

You're going to have fun with this chapter. But we're not going to start with you—not quite yet. Let's talk music for a moment. Let's talk about a musician you may never have heard of, but whose life lessons say a lot about your own life, believe it or not!

Earlier we quoted the legendary jazz player Charlie Parker, considered the greatest saxophonist of his generation. Less well known is the man who is considered the greatest player since Charlie Parker, an alto saxophonist named Art Pepper.

Pepper lived a difficult life, with bouts of drug abuse and prison time. Fortunately, the last few years of his life he got himself together and enjoyed his greatest success and triumphant tours. Even in his darkest days, the one thing that never failed him was his talent.

Pepper was in the worst depths of his drug abuse when he received a unique challenge—and an opportunity. He had been asleep, sickened by his addiction, when he was wakened by his producer. He had come to take Pepper to a recording gig with the band of the legendary Miles Davis, and—not surprisingly, considering his overall health and state of mind—Pepper had overslept. This might not be a problem for a healthy musician, but for Pepper it was critical. He didn't have time to get his drug fix—which he usually needed simply to get out of bed. He was going to have to play in his sickest, drug-neediest mode: half-conscious, physically ill, not even able to stand up. You would think that a disaster would ensue, right? Wrong!

The sessions that day became *Art Pepper Meets The Rhythm Section*, one of the most highly regarded jazz albums of all time.

Imagine if you had to go to work or take care of a child while desperately ill. How could you not only function, but excel, even have a truly legendary day?

You could only do so if your talent was so great that it just oozed out of you, regardless of how you felt. If it was so deeply ingrained in you that no obstacles or limitations—even self-imposed ones—could stop it from being expressed. If your talent was not only expressed, but *prevailing*!

Here is Art Pepper's explanation: "As for music, anything that I've done has been something done 'off the top.' I've never studied, never practiced. I'm one of those people: I knew it was there. All I had to do was reach for it, just do it...since the day I picked up the alto again I've realized that if you don't play *yourself* you're nothing. And since that day I've been playing what I felt, what *I* felt, regardless of what those around me were playing, or how they thought I should sound."

It's as if Art Pepper had read our book! He claims a unique talent and he sees just how unique that is to him. Now, he certainly was not functioning in all six dimensions of Intentional Difference—he certainly wasn't practicing to increase his mastery—but his life and talent as a saxophonist demonstrates with crystal clarity just how compelling our unique makeup is. Here again, lets look at the connection between the ID dimensions: our Critical Outcome is fueled by our Driving Passion; our Driving Passion is initiated by our Assimilated Experience; our Assimilated Experience is informed by our Cumulative Knowledge; our Cumulative Knowledge is expressed by our Emergent Skill; and our Emergent Skill, is fashioned by our Prevailing Talent.

Art Pepper's style and unique musical presentation was sculpted and molded by this thought, he said, "I've realized that if you don't play *yourself* you're nothing." Our Prevailing Talent—the spontaneous thoughts, feelings and behaviors—crafts, and fashions, as we see in Art's incomparable saxophone style how our unique Emergent Skill is expressed.

The six dimensions are like electrons in an atom. (see fig.1) They interact in a dynamic way to create, sustain and give of energy. Each of them are equally important and together, they produce the unique *difference* within us.

Figure 1

Okay, it's confession time. The three of us choose whether or not to answer our cell phones based on the name that pops up on the caller ID screen.

Of course, you would never do that, would you? Ha! Didn't think so!

But it's true! We may not answer in the moment, may delay listening to a voice mail or making a callback—all because of the name on the screen.

It's not that we prefer the name "Bill" to the name "Mary." It's that we experience the person represented by the name in a particular way that makes us feel eager, indifferent, obliged or hesitant to answer the phone.

Let's take it a step further. We are either the kind of person who often screens calls or does so only rarely, like when the house is on fire! And even one step beyond that—OUR name represents something to people on a caller ID screen too. Ever think of that?

So why the analogy? Because the caller ID phenomenon illustrates clearly the final dimension of Intentional Difference. It illustrates Prevailing Talent.

Remember our definition? Prevailing Talent is our *spontaneous, observable, reliable, and measurable patterns of thinking, feeling, and behaving*.

Back in the Introduction we mentioned a few of the many instruments widely used by corporations, counselors, and individuals—instruments like the Myers-Briggs Type Indicator©, the DiSC© profile, Clifton StrengthsFinder©, and CoreClarity©. In our work as consultants we use these extensively. The intent is to identify recurring patterns—or "talents" as we call them.

What's interesting is that most of us can intuitively recognize many of the recurring talents of others. "Nicolette always asks the right question at the right time." "Jennifer always knows how to get the best out of others." "Jim is always the guy you can count on to marshal resources and get a project going." "Miranda always makes others feel better about themselves."

Back to Art Pepper. Jazz critics said things like this about him: "He always comes up with an innovative lick." "He always brings out creativity in his bandmates."

But it's not till you hear what he had to say about his own artistry that you get his true unique Prevailing Talent.

Here's an example. One of his most famous recordings is a cover of "Somewhere Over the Rainbow," the famous song from *The Wizard of Oz.* But when you listen to it for the first time you might not recognize the tune. What's going on? Go ahead, listen to it. In fact, turn it up, close your eyes and listen to every note, every instrument and every breath.

Well, Art Pepper believed that his unique talent was to express the emotional undertone and meaning of a song, not just the melody and rhythm. His Prevailing Talent—what he did again and again in his career no matter what else was going on in his life—was to capture emotion in his playing. Both the emotion of the song itself and his own emotion. Listen to enough of his stuff and you experience it repeatedly. You may not hear the song you expect—

See Art Pepper video
http://bit.ly/14eIk6W
Once you have a QR code reader, place your smart phone over the QR code above.

the song Judy Garland made so famous. But you will hear *something.* You will hear emotion—and you will hear Art Pepper. He doesn't sound like anyone else!

If you are married, you've probably seen that you can predict whether or not your spouse will like a new song or television show without having to process carefully through your reasons why—you know the unique individual they are just on an intuitive level.

On the other hand, sometimes these recurring talents are harder to see in ourselves. That's why the testing instruments are so popular and why the book StrengthsFinder 2.0 spent so many weeks atop the business book best-seller lists.

These instruments are great—remember, we use them ourselves. But we have uncovered an even deeper and richer way of thinking about our Prevailing Talent that, when combined with the other five dimensions of Intentional Difference, can be a personal game-changer for you. Let's get to it by breaking down our definition.

Talent is *spontaneous.* It is a natural outflow of how we are wired. Like many of the other five dimensions it is expressed even when we don't realize what we are doing. You don't necessarily plan to do something out of your Prevailing Talent. Why? Because you couldn't stop yourself from doing it even if you wanted to—its automatic!

Talent is also *observable, reliable, and measurable.* How we talk, act, think, and interact with others is seen clearly by others, for the most part, and is easily predictable. We give off cues and clues to others about how we view the world through our speech patterns, thought processes, and ways of relating.

People know if you are going to be first or last to a party. If you have the mind of an engineer they know that you are going to tend to try to solve problems rather than offer empathy. If you have a talent for encouraging others, they know they may have to go elsewhere for brutally honest feedback. You are so you!

And talent is about the ways we *think, feel, and behave.*

Sometimes we tend to believe that thinking and feeling are opposites and that behavior is only vaguely related to the other two. To the contrary, they are intimately related. Our thinking can influence our feeling and vice versa, and our behavior tends to be a combination of how thinking and feeling work in concert.

But there is no cookie-cutter way of predicting this. You feel and think differently than others and your behavior is different because of this. There is something different about you and it has a lot to do with your Prevailing Talent.

Here's another wonderful thing about your Prevailing Talent—it actually *energizes* you.

All of us have an "energy account." Some of things that we do deplete our energy account. These are things we feel that we have to do, but that we derive no joy from doing. They don't draw on our passions or our Intentional Difference.

Part of our dream is that you will be inspired to organize your life in a way that you are doing less of those things that deplete your energy account, but the fact is that they are part of life. We will always have a certain amount of those items on our to-do list.

But when you are operating using your Prevailing Talent, you are actually making deposits into your energy account! Why?

Because your Prevailing Talent is a natural expression of who you are, how you are wired, how you think, and how you process experiences. When you exercise your Prevailing Talent you are expressing how you were made different to make a difference and this can't fail to bring you energy!

It's time for an exercise to make this real and personal to you. So pour a cup of coffee or tea, maybe put on some jazz, relax, and dive into the Energy Exercise!

The Energy Exercise
Think about the last time you went home at the end of the day happy and full of energy. If you work at home, think about the last time the

sun went down and you were more full of energy than when the day had started.

- What had you done that day?
- What particular talents that you have were you tapping into that day?

Think about the last time you went home at the end of the day drained and exhausted, maybe even a little depressed. If you work at home, think about think about the last time the sun went down and you were listless and exhausted and relieved that the day was almost over.

- What had you done that day?
- What particular talents that you have were you tapping into that day?
- What particular talents that you have were you NOT tapping into that day?

So far on our voyage, we have made it to our first major landfall—the six dimensions of ID. You have made some discoveries about the unique outcome you produce, the passion that drives you, the experience(s)that have shaped you, the type of things that you learn easily, the skill that naturally emerges from you, and the unique way that you think. Now where do we travel to from here? Well, what's a voyage without clear turquoise blue waters, pink powdery sandy beaches and cool tropical breezes? We go to the Bahamas, mon!

CHAPTER NINE

What's Your ID:

YOUR PERSONAL CHOICE?

W e were sitting under a cabana, on a beach, palm trees swaying and cool breeze blowing, sipping on a frozen concoction with a colorful umbrella in it, listening to this story: "One day I was in the Leonardo Da Vinci Airport," says Karen, the story teller. "I had just arrived from Paris and was about to exit the security area. I froze." As she says those words, she freezes mid-motion to illustrate her point. Then obviously reliving the event, with a terrified look on her face she continued her story. "My heart sank. My breathing became shallow. I began shaking all over… a realization hit me full force. I had just walked off and left a package I was carrying in a public bathroom stall! I began backing away from the exit. In a daze, overcome by the sheer reality of the costly error I had just made, I heard myself saying, 'No, no, no, oh no.' The armed security personnel standing nearby also heard me. I was immediately surrounded by guards each intent upon subduing me should I make a wrong move."

Karen didn't care. Not that the guards were ready to grab her. Nor that she looked like a crazy person—or worse. "I turned to them, and almost screaming I said, "I have to go back, I have to go back!" At this point in her story, Karen paused, her eyes brimming with tears at the memory. "What had just happened," Karen said as she recovered her emotions, "was, I had left a bright yellow bag containing a Picasso painting worth, at the time, $1,390,000 in a public bathroom stall. I had been commissioned to transport this one of a kind piece of art, and I had lost it."

Wait! You say. Roll back tape. Lets get our bearings here. Who is this person who has access to historical and priceless works of art? No one whose name you would know, but somebody that we were privileged to meet and recruit to join us on the voyage to discover and optimize her ID.

We were on the island of Eleuthera, in The Bahamas, having breakfast at the Buccaneer Restaurant, a favorite place of ours, when we noticed a woman who was not one of the regulars cleaning the tables. We were curious so we asked our server, a lovely woman named Pat, about the new employee. That's when she introduced us to Karen the daughter of the owner of the restaurant. As we chatted with Karen, who is a wonderful storyteller, we were reminded once again of how people can go through life as a functional but frustrated person because they are unaware of and un-intentional with their difference.

Karen Johnson was such a person, living a productive but unfulfilled life prior to discovering her ID.

Christened Katherine Elizabeth Johnson, born to Brenda and John Baldwin Johnson on the island of Eleuthera, Karen—as she is called by her friends and family—facilitates negotiations for the sale, purchase, and delivery of historical art items from her home base in Rome, Italy. In her own words, when we asked her what is she known for? she replied, "I am known to get things done, I am decisive and demanding, I deliver where others have failed to deliver." What a brand!

A brand that has positioned Karen as a go-to person for art collectors from New York, to Milan, Zurich and all around the world. She has helped to facilitate the transfer of ownership of diverse treasures, including one-of-a-kind swords, tiaras, and paintings, such as the Picasso painting.

It was this 'I get things done" mindset, no doubt, that Karen used to convince the authorities to shut down a section of the Leonardo Da Vinci airport until she was able to rescue the painting, personally signed "*To my friend Yul Bryner, P. Picasso,*" from the bathroom stall where she had left it.

As we continued our idDiscover© process with Karen we asked her, "What drives you?" "I believe there is a right way, a level of excellence at which things should be done!" She replied. "This is probably the one quality that causes me the most problems in life and in my work. I work mostly with men, rich and powerful men. I find that they are not used to a person like me."

We asked her to explain. "I'm a woman. I am black. I'm adamant. And I challenge the status quo. I refuse to let things be done at a mediocre level. I do not settle for good enough. So, many times I am called a 'witch' with a B, if you know what I mean. Truth is I wish I was different, that I could be less demanding, softer around the edges." We assured her that she was already perfectly different as she was meant to be, and that we would teach her how to be intentional with that difference.

Then we asked her, What experience has impacted your life? What specific instance or event has shaped you?

"That's a hard one," she replied at first. Then after some thought, she continued, "the instance that pops into mind, happened right here on this island when I was around 13 or 14 years old.

"I was visiting the home of a family friend, Dr. Sands, when I made what back then seemed like the unfounded and impulsive remark of a teenager." Here she begins to relate another one of the many incredible stories we heard over a two-day period. Stories at times so fantastic that as researchers we were compelled to validate them—to "fact check" what she was telling us. Every one of them, we discovered through our investigation is true. But back to the story Karen told us:

"I was standing there in the front room of this friend's home looking at 24 paintings, some on the wall, others hanging from the ceiling and still more spread neatly on the floor. They were for me mesmerizing. I was emotionally moved the moment I saw them. I turned to my uncle Lawrence and told him to buy them. Buy every one of them I said. The asking price was $5,000 for the lot. My uncle heard me, but in a culture where kids were expected to be seen and not heard, he ignored my plea. I don't know how or why, but even then as a teenager, I instinctively recognized exquisite and priceless works of art."

Karen was right, as she goes on to explain. "The paintings were by then unknown, but now renowned, Bahamian artist Amos Ferguson. His paintings range today anywhere from $5,000 each and up from there. My uncle later told me that he regretted not taking my advice decades prior." We asked Karen how that experience has shaped her. She said, "I learned from that experience and others just like it, that when it comes to works of art, I can trust my gut instinct."

Many of Amos Ferguson's originals were painted with house paint on discarded card board. You can see his art at www.harbourislandgallery.com/artists/ferguson.htm

This gut instinct that Karen has is true of the very best art critics, according to Malcolm Gladwell in his book *Blink*. In this book Gladwell introduces the idea of "Thin-slicing." It is knowing that you know. According to his theory, you may not know why or how you know, but you know instinctively and convincingly that you know. He describes it as the unconscious accumulation of knowledge over time. He says that each person's brain uniquely captures and stores specific bits of information in such a way that makes particular data more readily accessible, according to the person. The best art critics, like the rest of us, are constantly bombarded with millions of bits of data, Gladwell says. What differentiates the best art critics—indeed the best of the best in any field—is unique wiring that sifts through the daily deluge of data and highlights for easy recall data that is pertinent to their area of expertise.

Like others in our experience, Karen has an emergent skill, that uncanny ability which gushes out of her naturally. She told us another story, "I am at an art dealers event in Northern Italy, it's about one hour into the transaction in a bank where paintings were held in trust for the former king of Egypt. In the room is the bank manager, an art critic, a former professor from Saborn University and the Louvre, and a woman who was there to collect an original Gauguin painting that had been willed to her by the deceased king. As the painting was taken out of its protective packaging, we were all admiring the painting. I looked at the painting and before I could stop myself, I blurted out, 'It's a fake!'"

The room was shocked into silence. The art critic and the professor were utterly taken aback. Their first response was to rebut my claim. But upon closer examination, they too saw reason for further investigation. Eventually after weeks of thorough investigation it was discovered that the original had been replaced sometime ago with the fake one prior to the painting being placed into the vault at the bank."

Leaning in, we were deeply inquisitive, "What is this unique skill you have? When did you first notice it in your life?" We asked Karen to give us her answers.

"I was standing in a classroom in my old high school in Nassau. The Principal was giving me a tour of the art that students had produced. We looked at a number of art projects that the students had completed that were now on display. As we looked I noticed painted portraits that were a step above the rest, so I asked about them. The Principal said those are examples that we have used for years to show our students what very good painting structure and form looks like. I asked the principal who did the paintings. She replied that it was a student from many years ago, a young woman named Karen Johnson.

"It was only then that I realized that those were my paintings," Karen continues. "It was the only time I had done any painting and did not consider myself an artist of any sort. Yes, I can spot and detect great works by artists. But I have never thought of myself as one."

"So Karen," we asked, "What does this say about you?"

"I don't know, I have never given it much thought," she answered, shaking her head in bewilderment. "It's just what I do, who I am."

And it is who she is, and in your own unique way it is who you are, because you are so you!

"Thing is," Karen continued, "I have been so frustrated for such a long time. My frustration had become so intense that I decided to take this three month vacation back home."

Then with tears in her eyes she said, "I realized something during our conversation over these past two days. I have been living my life on automatic pilot. I have not been intentional at all—mostly I have been reactive. You are an answer to prayer."

Pausing to catch her breath and dry her eyes, she continued, "Just before I left Italy, a friend of mine saw me on the steps of the Basilica. He held my hands and said to me, "Katherine, Katherine, (he uses my formal name Katherine instead of Karen). I know that you are very confused and frustrated. But, I am praying that God will send someone to help you understand *you* clearer. This is amazing that I would go through this process—this conversation, at this time on this trip. This changes everything for me. I am going back to Italy with a clear sense of purpose. Thank you for helping me understand that I do not have to live my life by default—on automatic pilot, I can be intentional—intentional with my difference."

The bad news is that most people are still where Karen was, living their lives by default. The good news is that nobody has to live that way. We can all turn off the automatic pilot and become more intentional. And, we can increase our effectiveness and our level of success, by learning how to use what is different about us, in a purposeful, productive and determined way.

So what about you? Are you ready to move from automatic to intentional? Do you know your Intentional Difference?

Karen knows her Intentional Difference—and she can articulate it in one word....

CHAPTER TEN

What's Your ID:
YOUR ONE WORD?

I t's true—we left you hanging at the end of the last chapter. We needed to do that in order to be sure that we have your full attention. For we are about to reveal in this chapter how you can come to know your idWord—the *one word* that articulates the difference in you. It is not a word that you choose from a list of words. You won't find it by looking in a dictionary or a thesaurus, because your idWord is in you, has been in you for a long time. Right now, STOP reading, put down this book and get online at www.idDiscoveronline.com to discover your One Word.

Go to
idDiscoverOnline.com
to discover YOUR
idWord.
Once you have a QR
code reader, place your
smart phone over the
QR code above.

96

Now that you have your idWord, how do you optimize your intentional difference?

We spent a lot of time on Chris Gerdes's story in the first chapter for a reason—his story illustrates what happens when a person not only discovers his or her ID but also begins to OPTIMIZE their Intentional Difference.

What do we mean by "optimize"?

You are optimizing your ID when you are selectively putting your difference to use.

You see, each of us has the choice to live in one of three zones.

The first zone is the Distraction Zone. This is where we have not yet discovered our ID and so we spend a lot of our time doing the 85% activities we mentioned in the first chapter. These are those things that appear urgent but are in fact not things utilizing our unique ID—anybody can do these tasks. Remember, you were made different to make a difference, but until you have discovered your ID it's awfully hard to live that out.

The second Zone is the Leverage Zone. This is the zone where you are beginning to optimize your ID, like Chris Gerdes, Jeff Olszewski, Karen Johnson, and hundreds of others. Your idWord is the explicit expression of who you are. Knowing it empowers you to own and operate within your purpose. You begin to seamlessly operate within your six dimensions. Calling upon each one as you make proactive choices about your life, effortlessly responding to challenges and obstacles.

In naming your idWord you start to make the life-changing move from living automatically to living intentionally!

The third zone is the Flow Zone, which is the subject of the next chapter. For the moment, let's talk about what you are doing when you are in the Leverage Zone.

You are seeing connections, like Chris does…

1. I lost a friend in a car accident so I leverage my gifts as an engineer, critical thinker and problem-solver to lead teams working for breakthroughs in driver and passenger safety.
2. I had a great mentor who cared about students and this helped me, so now I pay it forward, which I am already naturally inclined to do anyway.
3. I realized in an undergrad class the value of collaboration in lifting the whole group to individual success, so I use the word collaboration dozens of times a day at the racetrack and, more to the point, I am a pacesetter in actually collaborating.

Chris isn't playing a role here. He's not applying technical ideas from the latest business book or motivational speaker, throwing a bunch of stuff against the wall and hoping something sticks.

He is making a difference because he is leveraging how he was made differently. He is leveraging his six dimensions. He is beginning to optimize his Intentional Difference!!

And so can you.

The Optimizing Exercise

In the space below, write the best short summary you can of the six dimensions of your ID, as you have discovered them on this voyage. Underneath each summary answer the provided question about how you have been intentional about each of those in the last 10 days (this is leveraging). And then write a statement of purpose—an intentional declaration, if you will—about how you will be even more intentional about that dimension in the next 10 days. Have fun, and get ready to enter the Leverage Zone as you become a world-class Optimizer!

Critical Outcome

Summary of my Critical Outcome:

How I have been intentional around this dimension in the last 10 days:

How I will be intentional around this dimension in the next 10 days:

Driving Passion

Summary of my Driving Passion:

How I have been intentional around this dimension in the last 10 days:

How I will be intentional around this dimension in the next 10 days:

Assimilated Experience

Summary of my Assimilated Experience:

How I have been intentional around this dimension in the last 10 days:

How I will be intentional around this dimension in the next 10 days:

Cumulative Knowledge

Summary of my Cumulative Knowledge:

How I have been intentional around this dimension in the last 10 days:

How I will be intentional around this dimension in the next 10 days:

Emergent Skill

Summary of my Emergent Skill:

How I have been intentional around this dimension in the last 10 days:

How I will be intentional around this dimension in the next 10 days:

Prevailing Talent

Summary of my Prevailing Talent:

How I have been intentional around this dimension in the last 10 days:

How I will be intentional around this dimension in the next 10 days:

CHAPTER ELEVEN

What's Your ID:

YOUR STRENGTHS OR WEAKNESSES?

In 1984, Michael Jordan wasn't yet "Michael Jordan"—the internationally known sports superstar.

In 1984, he had just finished a short but stellar college career in North Carolina. He was a star there from the first: as a freshman he hit the game-winning shot in the NCAA national championship game. But now he was ready to move to the big leagues—he had just been drafted by the Chicago Bulls of the NBA.

Dutifully, he boarded a flight to Chicago's O'Hare Airport, deplaned, collected his bags and got out. And waited for the ride the Bulls had promised him. And waited.

And waited.

Back in North Carolina, Michael Jordan had been a star. But here in Chicago, he was just another new guy. And the Bulls had forgotten to send a driver.

Fortunately, George Koehler—another young hopeful—was there, too. George wasn't an athlete. He was a young limo driver with a fleet of exactly one car, and he, too, had been forgotten. In fact, while Michael Jordan was waiting for his ride, George was also waiting—hoping against hope to find the customer who had booked his services, but who had never showed up.

A basketball fan, he recognized Jordan, gave up waiting for the other customer and offered the young star a ride.

During the 80's they would have made quite the unusual pair—Michael tall black and famous, and George—average-height, white and unknown limo driver. But, they have been best friends ever since and today journalists say that if you want to know where Michael is or get Michael on the phone you need to call George first. They are almost always together, either in Charlotte, where Jordan is the owner of the NBA's Bobcats (soon to be Hornets) or in Florida, where he has built a palatial estate.

Here's what George told ESPN: "I've met just about everyone under the sun through Michael. If you picked up a book about Michael's life, it would be my life, just Michael's name on the cover."

George Koehler was "lucky" enough to be there that day, you might surmise. Lucky enough to see the future "Michael Jordan" as a confused and slightly intimidated young kid from coastal North Carolina without a ride (and before cell phones!) outside of one of the world's busiest airports.

In a moment in time, George gave Michael Jordan a ride and since then he has had a front row seat to the greatest career in basketball history and a lifestyle of privilege and achievement. He knows the rich and famous, has been personally successful, and has unlimited traveling privileges aboard Jordan's Gulfstream IV jet, which was built to resemble a basketball sneaker, complete with Jordan's personal "Jumpman" logo.

Lucky, right?

But what if it wasn't luck at all?

What if what happened that day at O'Hare was really just the culmination of twenty-nine years of an Intentional Difference lived out, a climactic moment in time when George realized that his entrepreneurial bent, love of connecting with people, uncanny knack for seeing opportunities others were missing, and ability to quickly and thoroughly win the trust of others were coming together for this moment—this one great, life-altering opportunity?

And what if something similar could happen for you?

"What is the one thing you, as leaders, are custodians of?"

This was the question we asked a group of educators, many of whom are deans and chairs of departments at notable universities around the world. We got the usual answers we get when we ask this question at the beginning of our workshops. Some said, the organizations' resources. Others said, the people who report to us. Still others said, the vision and mission of the organization.

These were good answers, but they weren't complete. What we were looking for was something more all-encompassing. Something that saw the entire picture. We believe that leaders, regardless of the position they hold, are custodians of more than profits or mission. More than staffing tables or even the vision of their particular organization. We believe leaders are custodians of *potential*.

Whether you—or he or she—is a president, a parent, a teacher, a CEO or a manager, a leader is charged with and held accountable for turning potential into performance, performance into practice, and practice into a profitable outcome. A leader's success is measured by what he or she does with potential. The first step toward success as a leader is being able to spot potential. First your own and then that of others.

Most organizations are involved with identifying potential through some process. As we mentioned in the first chapter, organizations in their quest to flush out employee potential, use psychometric tools. Some of those organizations focus on what strengths an individual possesses. Others focus both upon the strengths and weaknesses an individual possesses. Looking at performance through the lens of strengths and/ or weaknesses limits our view of a person's potential. For speaking in terms of a person's strengths or weaknesses is a judgement about past performance that may or may not be true of their potential in the present depending on the situation. With this book, and through the ever-widening number of people who are discovering their ID through their articulated idWord, we hope to stop that thinking—to shift the focus from strengths or weaknesses, or strengths and weaknesses, and instead put the focus on the natural *difference* within each person. By doing this, then we can fully assess and tap into a person's potential— their capacity for excellence.

Our greatest potential lies in what is different about us. We unleash our potential by becoming intentional with that difference.

Intentional Difference is for everyone!

Throughout this voyage together, we've shared the stories of everyday people and famous folks. We've included a few people in between. But mostly, we've majored on the everyday folks because ID is not for an elite blessed with unusual brainpower or good looks or networked connections. ID is for all of us.

But right now, we are going to talk about a very famous and fabulously wealthy guy whom you may have heard of.

James Dyson is a British billionaire, industrial designer and founder of the Dyson Company. He is also an inventor best known for one invention. That, as you may know from the ads, is his famous Dyson

Dual Cyclone vacuum cleaner, a vacuum cleaner that unlike every other vacuum cleaner since the appliance was invented, moves and operates differently—it actually pivots on a ball and operates without a bag. The unique and brilliant design of the machine means that it never loses suction power. Millions of commercial cleaning workers and stay at home moms with a little extra spending money rise up and call James Dyson blessed!

He's invented many other things but today may be best known for his Dyson Foundation. The foundation encourages young people to become engineers and scientists, to be sure, but what's unique about it is, it actually encourages these same young people to make mistakes, and even incentivizes well-documented mistakes!

You see, James Dyson learned early on that the combination of failure and determination can [not necessarily will!] lead to great things. He wasn't a good athlete as a young man, but he excelled as a long distance runner simply because he was more determined than other kids.

And the very nature of his calling as an inventor would be that he refused to become discouraged as prototype after prototype bit the dust—he would simply keep going until he had THE product.

The product that makes you and I say, "Why didn't I think of that?"—THE product brilliant in its innovation, elegant in its simplicity.

But, that's just the point, right? You and I didn't invent it; James Dyson did! Because dogged determination and creative thinking are simply part of his Intentional Difference.

Here's what this famous inventor told the *Wall Street Journal* recently: "I don't like science fiction. I don't think it's very clever, to be honest. It's very easy to imagine what the world will be like. The difficult thing is making the world a better place and making things work better."

And that's it in a nutshell—"making the world a better place and making things work better." That's James Dyson's Intentional Difference.

It's not just that he has discovered the six dimensions of his ID. And it's not just that he has figured out how to leverage those strengths operating together by optimizing his ID.

No, James Dyson has figured out how to UNLEASH his ID, and it is with this powerful concept that we end this leg of our voyage together.

You may never become a billionaire or the irreplaceable assistant of an international celebrity. But the power of your Intentional Difference CAN be unleashed in your life. Through it you can make more of a difference than you may have ever dreamed—in your life and in the lives of those who matter the most to you!

This won't be the end of your voyage of Intentional Difference but when you do reach the point of unleashing, you'll notice the sea squalls and darkness will have lifted and you will have bright skies and bracing breezes and the excitement of an unparalleled and thrilling life voyage ahead!

The Flow Zone

Remember, in the last chapter we talked about the Distraction Zone (where you are mired in activities that are not part of your ID but are part of the 85% of what you are capable of doing that most anyone can do?). And we talked about the Leverage Zone, (or the 10% select others can be trained to do just as well as you) where you see how the six dimensions of your ID work together seamlessly.

Now, we're talking about your 5%, your Flow Zone.

"Flow" is not a new concept. Given a name by the psychologist Mihaly Csikszentmihalyi, flow describes that incredible experience where everything but the present moment falls away and you are totally and incredibly focused on excellence. And it's not trying to be excellent—you simply are fully present and invested in those moments.

You've heard the terms—"in the zone," "in the moment," "fully present."

It's when an actor *becomes* Henry VIII, rather just playing a role. It's when the hole looks 10 feet wide to a golfer about to attempt a match-winning putt. It's when a woman who mentors young girls understands precisely what they are saying—even when they aren't yet able to find the right words—and has the precisely right response, full of wisdom and kindness. It's when everything slows down and your actions are natural and unforced and *right*.

When Csikszentmihalyi was doing his original research for his work, he interviewed many men and women who had lived through these sorts of peak experiences and he found that they kept using the analogy of a water current carrying them along. The exact opposite of "going with the flow," which is doing what everyone else is already doing.

This experience was being carried along on a powerful current that was clean and bracing and clear and refreshing and incredible.

As Csikszentmihalyi continued his research, he saw that this experience transcended generations and even cultures.

When Michaelangelo painted the ceiling of the Sistine Chapel he would work in impossible conditions. Flat on his back, motionless except for his painting hand for days (!) at the time, giving up sleep, food, and even water, he would paint. Eventually, he would pass out. But then he would awaken, totally refreshed and energized, and continue painting.

You've been there, right—at least once in your life? An all-nighter for an exam you had to ace? A work project to which you were passionately committed? The pursuit of the love of your life?

What if you could go there a lot more?

You can.

You just have to unleash your Intentional Difference.

Remember the central idea of this book:

"You are made different to make a difference"

We believe that with our whole hearts and our experience bears it out.

We want this for our own lives and we want it for you.

Here is where ID gets unleashed…

When your idWord becomes branded into your soul. When your idWord is the name you discover within you for your Intentional Difference. This discovery is *your* discovery, not a paragraph, nor a list of labels, or themes, or types someone else has assigned to you. Your idWord is your noun for your identity. And once you arrive at your one word, that changes everything.

That September afternoon at a racetrack in California as Chris Gerdes rehearsed the key events of his life, his marker moments, his values through our idDiscover process he came up with his idWord:

VOYAGER.

And in the same way, on a pink sandy beach in The Bahamas so did Karen 'Katherine' Johnson. Her idWord:

PERFECTION.

In the future, we hope to share the follow up to Chris's and Karen's stories, as well as the stories of the others we mentioned in this book as they continue to discover more about how to begin to optimize, unleash and live out their idWord.

And we hope you will share your voyage of discovery to your Intentional Difference with us as well.

For now, and in full regard and affection for each of you, we briefly share our own stories of coming to our idWord.

Ken's ID Voyage:

People know me as an innovator, a thinker, a businessman. But I can be nervous, too. I was anxiously awaiting my time slot on the agenda at our partners meeting. The idea I was going to share was a game changer. I sat there imagining how the other partners would celebrate the opportunity to change our offerings to our clients while also establishing us as a key player among the giants in our industry. Not so. When my time came, I began to lay out my ideas. But I had barely spoken for five minutes when the room erupted with passionate resistance. People were booing. They were waving me down. I could not believe my eyes and ears. I was flabbergasted.

For the next forty-five minutes I tried different ways to deliver what I felt was a blue ocean strategy that would change our brand in the marketplace, to no avail. Emotions were running high, and the entire room seemed to be adamant against my idea. Someone suggested we take a five-minute break to cool down. While on break I noticed little pockets of two and three partners talking quietly together. I was not one of them, standing alone as I was. When we reconvened I opened the meeting by pointing out what I had observed, and I asked the members of these little conclaves to please share what the private conversations were about if they pertained to the subject at hand. They did, and this is what I learned and how I came to my idWord. They admitted they were upset not because my idea was not a good one, but because they felt blindsided, they felt ambushed by the sheer enormity of the idea!

"Oh," I said." You see it never occurs to me that usually I have an idea, move it to fruition and only then introduce it to those concerned. They told me what I do is disruptive…in a good way. It momentarily takes your breath away… like a quick Heimlich maneuver to the abdomen, intrusive but life-giving. That started me thinking and talking about this with my co-authors and other researchers working on this project. They encouraged me to apply our observations and our idDiscover process to myself.

The result—my idWord:

DISRUPTOR

That's me. It's not pretty. It may even sound negative to some. It's not. Like any other noun, it is neutral. Its all about....wait for it...being intentional with your difference. "Disruptor" is my unique identity, my 5%, my ID, the contribution I bring that adds value to any conversation. I shake up the status quo. I challenge what *IS* with the new idea of what *must* be. It is what my siblings remember about me as a kid. It's the brand I have from high school. It's what I did in college. It is what I do for clients everyday. What I do in my family. What I do for my partners. It is how I discovered and invented Intentional Difference. It is me, using *my* difference to make a difference.

Todd's ID Voyage:

Today, I am a pastor, management consultant, executive coach, and writer. But I used to be a toddler.

I know, profound.

"You ask so many questions!" they told me, even when I was a toddler.

But all toddlers ask questions, right?

Why is blue, blue? Why does candy taste sweet? Where do clouds come from? Why does Aunt Ruth have a beard?

That's what toddlers do. There's nothing special about being a questioning toddler.

As a kid and a teenager I liked all of the normal stuff—sports, pop culture and music, girls.

The things I enjoyed the most were co-editing the high school newspaper and serving as senior class president.

When I made my campaign speech for senior class president, the first words out of my mouth were in the form of a question: "Why do we have student government and do we really need it?"

My favorite student newspaper article (and classmates still make fun of me for it to this day) was about the installation of a new septic system on the campus. When I asked the director of facilities and maintenance for an interview he looked at me as if I were crazy. His look confirmed that he thought I was crazy when my first question was: "Given all of the competing priorities at this school right now, can you tell me why a new septic system is at the top of the list for capital expenditures?"

My favorite quote during those days was from a man whose views I repudiated, Friedrich Nietzsche: "A man can bear any 'how?' if he has a big enough 'why?'"

In college, my favorite professors were those who challenged my passionately held convictions. I couldn't stand people who thought they knew everything there is to know. I loved those who knew just how to ask the right, probing questions that called even their most deeply held views up to the light.

In my first ministry job, the team, on retreat, was asked to say something affirming about each team member. I longed to hear "He's so kind." Or "He is such a compassionate pastor." Or "He's so warm."

Instead, I heard "He always puts things in a fresh way and always asks questions that shed light."

In my first consulting job—a job in which I was WAY over my head—a much-more experienced colleague said to me, in front of others, "You always ask the perfect, probing question."

I started to see a pattern. But I didn't like it.

Who wants to be the one asking the questions, like some overgrown toddler?

Then I hit the deepest, darkest valley of my life, a time of personal failure and great loss. I talked to God. But, for the most part, I didn't rail at him. And I didn't indulge in the passing anesthesia of self-condemnation.

I asked questions. Lots of them.

A quote from my favorite author, Frederick Buechner, got me through this time: "Listen to your life. See it for the fathomless mystery it is."

I love mystery novels. And the best detectives in those novels are not the ones who know the answers somehow, as if they plucked them out of the air. No, the best detectives are the ones who know how to ask just the right questions at just the right time.

And then our concept of Intentional Difference began to develop and Ken, Shane, and I had to go on our own idVoyages if we were to have integrity as writers.

For some of our clients, the process of finding their idWord, of self-analysis is unusual, even uncomfortable. For some it is challenging and emotional. We honor those experiences.

For others, the process has been almost joyous and instantaneous.

I am one of the latter. My idWord:

QUESTIONER

I am a Question-Asker.

This fits like a pair of well-worn jeans or a favorite college sweatshirt.

I see life through the lens of questions rather than answers. This doesn't mean I don't think there are answers. It does mean the questions that lead up to the answers are of vital importance.

It's not about being a questioning toddler. It's about having confidence that whatever room I am in the very best value I can bring will in somehow relate to the questions I am raising. And I find incredible joy and satisfaction in that.

Shane's ID

Todd, Ken, and I were walking up to security at San Francisco International Airport to catch a flight to Santa Barbara, surrounded by a harried crowd of travelers trying to get to their destination. In the midst of these destination seekers (of which I have been one my whole life), we had a little different frame of mind. We were on a journey, together. We'd spent several days together writing, thinking, and interviewing people for this book. Todd and Ken, a half step ahead of me, turned and asked, "so what is it, Shane? What is your ID?"

As with most, I could easily identify what my 85% is —it is my distraction zone. I could rattle off a list of things that drained my energy. Activities I knew I could do, maybe even with some degree of proficiency, but none that really fueled me. I was even in a long-term career in which by all accounts you could say I was fairly successful. But, before I even knew it, I knew I wasn't grasping what my flow zone, my ID entailed. You know those moments you know you're not quite there, even when you don't totally know what there is? That's the way I was feeling. Moreover, that was the way I was living.

In a quick wave of activity, thoughts swirling around and flashback memories scrolling immediately before me like a slideshow on speed, I went back to a moment two years prior.

I was parked on a bench overlooking a beautiful lake at sunset on a warm February day in North Carolina. The sky was painted with rich colors that can only be experienced as the sun is setting. It was like pushing the pause button for a few minutes. Sometimes pause allows us to catch up to ourselves. I was there to do just that. Two days alone to seek clarity and respite.

For me, this is where my ID journey began, or at least became clearer. Like you, I probably never considered what I did and the way I did it, to be all that significant. I just did it.

Re-entry after pausing can be dangerous, so I was sitting in the study of my journey guide. He asked me this question, "Why do you do what you do?" Wow! I wasn't ready for that question. I thought about it a moment and responded, "Transformation. It's all about transformation for me. No matter what role I'm in, no matter where I do it, I want to make a difference and help people and organizations transform." Not all that unique is it? But that's where the clarity of my journey began. It wasn't in what I did, it was in me, how and why I did it. That was my Driving Passion, to make a transformational difference!

But it was that moment that launched a new journey for me.

Walking through the terminal I was wondering. "What am I known for?" Throughout my career I've never entered a role and filled someone's shoes. I've always been the guy that came into leadership positions and either started something new or transitioned the existing organization into new space. In fact, in my career, that's what I was known for. I would receive job offers based on what I had accomplished in other places. I spent 20 years building, cleaning up messes, and helping organizations write a new script and reframe their new reality. But I was never inclined to stick around too long. I got bored and felt the desire to move on.

A few more steps in the security line. I started reflecting on the experiences that have shaped me. You know those experiences that really did a number on me, like the hands of an artist on a tough piece of clay. The immediate ones—my dad's death when I was 15, my bouts with depression when I was 20. Meeting my wife, the birth of my daughters, the specific challenging times I faced in my career. The education system had all but given up on guys like me, who barely graduated high school, but I battled through, graduating from college with honors and moving onto a master's program at an Ivy League school and ultimately a doctorate.

As these and many more experiences started to assimilate into my life, they have made an indelible impression on me. Not just an impression on me, they are *me*—and they could be no one else.

As I thought about these experiences, I realized something else. During each episode, there was someone in my life to guide me though that season, a catalyst of sorts. Chuck Harris, Jennifer Roberson,

Herman Heluza, Tom Dabasinskas, Jim Osterhaus, Troy Simpson, Steve Freiburger, Leighton Ford … the list could go on and on.

As I started to recall the people who shaped me, I thought of Herman Heluza; a freshman English professor at a community college in California. He was the first guy who saw something in me no one else did. He found value in what I wrote. Others found errors and marked my papers up with red ink. He called me into his office one day and said, "Shane, there's a writer in you that has to come out. You have a unique perspective that you need to figure out how to describe. You're going to do great things if you only unleash what's inside of you." I always knew I saw the world a little different than others. Professor Heluza was a catalyst for me to own and affirm that about myself.

The way I'm wired is I see things, events, people, all with the end goal in mind. I live in the moment, love to vision and dream, am energized by complexities and thrive on getting to the simple side of complex. I see things the way they could be. That's when it hit me, my idWord:

CATALYST

That's my ID, my 5%. When I serve as a catalyst for transformational change for people, groups, organizations, that's when I'm in my 5%. I thought about it a moment or two. *Catalyst*. Hmmm… is that how I would characterize my ID?

So I thought I would try it out. Todd and Ken and I had made it through the lengthy security line. With them a step ahead, I blurted out, "Catalyst!" I kept walking, they stopped, and both simultaneously responded, "Yes, that's it!"

Then I ran it through the reflective lens of my life. It made sense, that's what I do, I am a catalyst to transition people, groups and organizations. I am a catalyst of new initiatives, new thoughts, new frames. I am a catalyst for new ideas. A catalyst for transformation.

CHAPTER TWELVE

What's Your ID:

MADE DIFFERENT TO MAKE A DIFFERENCE?

I n the last chapter we revealed the personal discovery of each of our idWords. Through painstaking introspection and our idDiscover© process we came to articulate our unique difference in one word. But, so what?

Is that the end of our journey? Are we done once we have our idWord? Not at all—just the opposite, because knowing your idWord is not a destination. It's an origination—a beginning—a gestalt moment. That instance when for the first time you see yourself, the world, your place in the world in a profoundly different way.

In that moment a cataclysmic event occurs, like a supernova deep within you that changes everything. It's an explosion of understanding—showering light down upon suppressed successes from which important lessons can now be gleaned; on opportunities missed that you will now pursue; on conflicts you handled in one way that you will now handle differently going forward; on relationships you may still have the opportunity to preserve and deepen with your now enriched self-awareness.

Discovery of your ID changes everything—it changes your perspective about life, work, relationships and purpose. It changes your understanding of YOU.

The way you understood you, until now, was mainly by the name you have been given. Your name and the choice your parents or others made for that name has some significance. In some cultures, the name you have been given, you were given because of the distinct meaning of the name in an original language. Angelo, in Greek means, messenger of God. In others the significance of a name given is in honor of an ancestor. Maybe you are named after a great aunt or your grand father. In some instances a name may be given simply because the parent heard the name somewhere and liked it as a name. The name Scarlett was popular right after the movie *Gone With the Wind* made its debut. Fact is, you were given a name. It may or may not have been given to you with profound thought and meaning. But you own your name as your unique identity. That name is you. It is your reality. As of February 2011, there were 1,057,723 persons in the USA who share the same name with Ken. They all spell their names the same. They are pronounced the same. The letters on a page or nametag are the same. The reality is not. We each have our own reality, our own lives, and our unique identity. We are different—but our given name does not embody that difference. However our idWord *does*—it identifies, clarifies and christens our unique Self.

Chris Gerdes whose story we wrote about at the beginning of this book, through his investment in students and his work on the autonomous vehicle, will be known for his contributions to driver-safety and higher education. He will be known for the historic driverless-car ride up Pike's Peak, and the coordinated rescue of the crashed helicopter occupants. However, he will be known best as VOYAGER, one who embarks on new adventures, assimilates the right people, leverages the best of what each person has to offer, and allows them to express their difference, intentionally!

Chris Gerdes video
http://bit.ly/1aQox2K
Once you have a QR code reader, place your smart phone over the QR code above.

His voyage is not completed. It is ongoing. No terminal destination. Looking back, our guess is that people will see the impact that his VOYAGER has made on their lives—the teams that he impacted, the businesses that he molded, the families that he shaped and the schools that he forged.

Chris's ID will be felt for years to come, as will yours, as will ours.

Remember what we observed through 65 years of studying people:

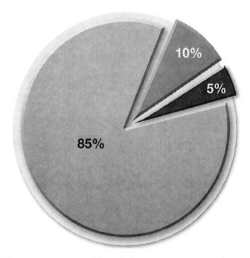

85% of what we are capable of doing, most people can do.

10% of what we are capable of doing, select people can be trained to do.

5% of what we are capable of doing, we alone are able to do it, the way *we* do it.

Your idWord names that 5%. It provides a way to describe in one word the characteristics of your difference. And it is your word—articulated and defined by you.

For us, our idWords, Questioner, Catalyst and Disruptor, capture the unique perspective, value and contribution which we bring to each situation—they provide a way for us to own our difference, our 5%. Kelly Jasen, Client Relations Manager at TAG Consulting reveals her idWord and tells us how she sees that discovery impacting her going forward:

"Paying the Mortgage. That's what I have to keep in mind today. Paying the mortgage." My friend posted this on Facebook yesterday, which is surprising to me because she's brilliant, accomplished, educated and overall, amazing. She's an excelling Microsoft executive and she is going to work every day just to get the mortgage paid.

Yet how often have I found myself in a similar role? Indeed, how many of us have that same thought virtually every day at work? We are doing what we do because we need to do it to get the paycheck at the end of the day. We might not hate our work, but we also don't love it, feel energized by it, look forward to it. Is it a surprise then that 7 out of 10 employees consider themselves disengaged or actively disengaged?

My passion is to change that statistic. To change the workplace. To change my role, your role, his role, her role … to change the organization itself … to no longer yield to status quo or surrender to dissatisfaction but to work with individuals and organizations to be engaged employers with engaged employees (who incidentally happen to then be 6 times more successful than their competitors!).

I know this is what I want to pursue because I know my ID.

I know my *Intentional Difference* is to use my talents, my skills, my passion, my experiences, and my knowledge to make a difference in the workplace and to impact individuals and organizations to be more. By knowing what my difference is, I can figure out the "So what?" and the "Now what?" I can figure out and choose how to use my *Dumbledore* in ways to make a difference.

When I first did my ID and came up with my "word." I was momentarily excited, even impassioned by it. "I'm Dumbledore!" But shortly thereafter, I started thinking, "well what the heck does that mean?"

"Dumbledore", my ID word, is not a destination.

It's a beginning. It allowed me to know more about who I am, who I want to be, what I'm good at, what I'm passionate about, and how to put all of that together to know what I can do, the 5% I can do that no one can do, and then to start dreaming big about how to do just that. Whoa that's a run-on sentence, but I got a little excited there!

I am going to use my ID, my *"Dumbledore"* to transform the workplace. Next year I might want to use my ID to launch races across the Mohave Desert or paint every single street light post in America purple. Who knows? But I get to focus on what I love and what I'm good at, and that makes all the difference so I can make a difference wherever I go."

Like Kelly says, knowing your idWord is a beginning not a destination. And for Kelly and hundreds like her, for you and us, and millions more to come, the discovery of our idWord immediately reinvigorates and infuses life with energizing hopefulness. It feels good. It's liberating to finally and fully accept that your quirkiness, your idiosynchronies, your brand of creativity, is exactly what you need to succeed. But, again as Kelly says, "So what? Now what?"

Now you begin making a difference with your difference by using your idWord to identify your 5%. Identifying your 5% is the same as recognizing your potential—your capacity for excellence. So what is your potential? What does your 5% look like? It looks just like your idWord suggests:

My (idWord) suggests I like to _____

My (idWord) suggests I need to _____

My (idWord) suggests I prefer to _____

My (idWord) suggests I dislike _____

My (idWord) suggests I yearn to _____

My (idWord) suggests that I oftentimes _____

My (idWord) suggests I insist on _____

My (idWord) suggests I avoid _____

My (idWord) suggests I am unlikely to _____

My (idWord) suggests I am most fulfilled _____

Okay, so now you have a list of charteristics which describe your 5%—your potential. Now put it aside. You do not need the list now. You know instinctively what you idWord means to you. You know it fully with all of its charteristics immediately upon thinking of it. It is your word. And upon naming it, *you got it.* It's yours forever, wherever and whenever. The key is to apply what you now know and own intentionally in every situation. So lets look at the various areas of your life and see how you can turn your potential into performance. Try the following:

I. USE YOUR IDWORD TO IDENTIFY YOUR 5% ZONE: Your ID comes with built-in cues for success. You have an innate need to achieve certain milestones in your career based upon your ID. For some people the measurement may be job promotions—climbing the corporate ladder. For others it may be technical certifications—becoming known as an expert in your field. For others it may be achieving a certain income level—receiving the maximum percentage salary increase allowed each year. Whatever your success metrics are for your career or life, here is how you can use your ID to identify your 5% zone:

1. Based upon how you understand your idWord, (page 138) make a list of at least five tasks within your role you are already good at that you believe you can be great at.

2. Make another list of tasks you are average at, that you believe you can become good at.

3. And yes, you know it, make a list of tasks you are mediocre or poor at.

4. From the lists above, which tasks are critical to your role?

   a._____

   b._____

   c._____

   d._____

   e._____

5. Now for each task you listed above answer this question: "To what degree and in what way does my ID help me to get this task done?"

6. List the tasks where you know your ID empowers you to do an excellent job (this is your 5% zone in this role).

7. List the tasks where you know your ID helps you to do an average job. (This is your 10% zone).

8. For each item on the list that you feel your ID does not help to get the task done, (your 85% zone) try to develop a process that helps you to get the task done.

9. For each activity where you are unable to develop a process, identify a partner, someone who does this task well (their 5% zone) to help you get the task done.

II. USE YOUR IDWORD TO ENHANCE RELATIONSHIPS: Any time you walk into a new space you make an impact. The atoms that make up your physical being is introduced into that space and immediately they begin interacting with the atoms already in the room. Its unconscious, invisible and undetectable, but it happens. So also is the case with your ID and that of the other person. In each interaction with someone, our differences are doing a dance. Your opportunity is to turn each such occasion into a beautifully flowing waltz. Here's how to do that:

1. Before meeting with the person with whom you want to enhance your relationship conduct a personal audit of that relationship by writing a short statement of how you believe the other person views you:
    a. What are you known for by them?
    b. How have they seen you demonstrate your driving passion?
    c. How has your experience with others, who are in ways similar to them, impacted your interaction with them?
2. Now think of your idWord, look at the list of suggestions or characteristics you wrote earlier on page 138.
    a. Select the characteristics you know have had a positive impact upon this person.
    b. Do the same with the ones you know have had a negative impact upon this person.
    c. Based upon the above determine the appropriate action you will take to enhance the relationship.

III. USE YOUR IDWORD TO MAKE CAREER CHOICES: We make thousands of choices every day. Big ones, small ones, ones with lasting impact, ones with fleeting impact. But one of the most important set of choices we make are those impacting our careers. We spend at least 10 hours out of every weekday doing things that pertain to our jobs. Put those hours into percentage of waking hours per week and we spend forty-five percent of the time we are awake on things related to our work. Almost half of your conscious life is impacted by the choices you make regarding your career. Right now think of your idWord and what it says about you in your present role? How's that working for you?

At one time, the Gallup organization queried employees 18 years old and older about the question, "I have the opportunity to do what I do best everyday." Seventy-percent of people responded they did not have such an opportunity in their careers. That's seven out of 10 persons in jobs where they were not presently using their difference to make a difference! They were going to work everyday, spending valuable waking-life hours on automatic pilot! No need for you to do that. You know your Intentional Difference, use that data to make better career choices. Here's how:

1. Compare the requirements of the job with the characteristics of your idWord.
   Is there obvious alignment/misalignment?
2. Will the culture of the organization allow you to be (circle one):
   Fully you?
   Satisfactorily you?
   Minimally you?
3. Based upon your ID what will your performance likely be in this role?
   Finish this statement if you can, "In this role (the role under consideration) I am (put your idWord here) by that I am likely to perform (put your estimation of your performance level)
IV. USE YOUR IDWORD TO LIVE DAILY IN YOUR PURPOSE: Nothing changes everything as surely as owning your purpose. Do it now! Live your purpose right now in the present conversation, in the

present interaction, through the task you are presently doing. Do it now by being aware of the purpose embodied within your idWord. People often speak about purpose in terms of a visionary big event. We do the same. For instance, we say, our purpose is to change the world. That is what we feel, what we strive to do. But if we are not intentional, our purpose can seem and feel like something that is distant, something that may be fulfilled sometime in the future. But, with your idWord in mind, you can live your purpose in the present—moment by moment. Here's how:

1. IN THE MORNING—GET FULLY DRESSED: While you are shaving or fixing your hair, or putting on make-up or whatever you do to get prepared physically for your day—get mentally prepared as well. Look anew at the characteristics of your idWord and let that inform and direct you as to the purpose for your life. Rick Warren, in his best selling book *The Purpose Driven Life*, says, "Without a clear purpose you have no foundation on which you base decisions, allocate your time, and use your resources." So, get dressed in your idWord and live today with your purpose clearly in mind.

2. DURING YOUR DRIVE TO WORK—CHECK YOUR DASHBOARD: Good drivers are aware moment by moment of each dial on their dashboard. As you drive through the workday check often to ensure your automatic pilot switch is turned OFF and your ID switch is turned ON, purposefully. Do this because the quality of your productivity today and everyday will depend upon how much time you spend in automatic–no-thought-given–to-your-uniqueness-mode, versus the time you spend being intentional with your difference.

3. ON THE DRIVE HOME—USE YOUR REAR-VIEW MIRROR: Reflect on the day. How well did you live your purpose

today? What were the instances when you were most intentional? What were the results? How often were the instances when you were not intentional? At the end of the day, what lessons did you learn about your purpose today? What steps will you take to live your purpose more fully tomorrow?

V. USE YOUR IDWORD TO IMPROVE COMMUNICATION EFFECTIVENESS: Your ID is like your own personal litmus test…it is sensitive to those communication events for which you are more or less equipped. The single most cited reason for family, classroom, team, or organizational discontent is ineffective communication. No matter the relationship, people struggle to effectively communicate. Being intentional about effective communication is to exercise our ID in a manner that brings clarity, instills trust, and creates forward movement. First, you have to honor your own ID. When we honor something, we intentionally cultivate its growth and health. Facing a difficult conversation, having troubles communicating, or feeling like your dialogue with others is stalled? Try this:

1. CULTIVATE AWARENESS—BOTH IN SELF AND OF OTHERS. We are not always even nominally aware of what we bring into our interactions with others. Start paying attention to your own ID as expressed in each of the six dimensions. Forge a new depth of understanding of how each dimension impacts the other. Then start to look for and listen for how others' dimensions are expressed. Awareness brings clarity!

2. CHOOSE RESPECT—FOR THE OTHER PERSON OR PEOPLE. Everyone craves a little bit of "R.E.S.P.E.C.T.," just ask Aretha Franklin. Respect is a choice. Awareness of self and others leads us to make the choice to respect others for what they contribute to a conversation, a team, a family, classroom or

an organization. You can choose to respect someone for their difference, not labeling them, but honoring what they are best at and allowing them to freely express their ID.

3. INSTILL TRUST—WHO YOU SEE IS WHAT YOU GET. When we optimize and unleash our ID, we offer the best of who we are for the world. The consistency of that offering instills trust in people, and establishes your credibility. Effective communication is not just about what you say or how you say it. It's about who you are and how you deliver you, intentionally. Take your idWord and be intentional about how that word would communicate to other people in a productive, trust-building manner. Consider how your idWord may, if experienced negatively, be a roadblock to your communication effectiveness. What about your application needs to be altered? It's not about changing you, but the intentional application of your approach. The cumulative effect of Awareness, Respect, and Trust is forward movement. Don't add another mechanism to communicate more effectively. Work with your raw material, you! Be intentional with your *you-ness*.

VI. USE YOUR IDWORD TO NAVIGATE CONFLICT: Conflict is your ally. That is what Joe Jurkowski, James Osterhaus, and Todd Hahn posit in their book *Thriving Through Conflict*. What we have come to discover in our work is each of us has our triggers. Buttons get pushed, levers get pulled, hot spots of pain get unearthed. What if conflict is more about two people intentionally expressing their difference. Take a Disruptor and a Catalyst for example. The two can be a powerful positive force, like two cylinders of an engine firing in perfect spontaneity. The two can also create sparks. Here's how to turn friction into productive energy:

1. MAKE SPACE: Allow room for people to express their ID, even if it's not how you would say it, do it, or see it. Be sure you're being authentic and intentional yourself.

2. BORROW THE OTHER PERSON'S EYES: Consider what life is like on the other side of you. The resistance we face in the midst of conflict actually gives us insight into how we come across to others because of our ID.

3. MAKE CONFLICT YOUR ALLY: Be Intentional about learning from each conflict opportunity. Conflict teaches us about our Critical Outcome, triggers our Driving Passion, surfaces our Assimilated Experience, utilizes our Cumulative Knowledge, at times propels our Emergent Skill and is informed by our Prevailing Talent. Perform a Monday-morning quarterback routine. After the energy around the conflict has subsided, do a post-conflict read on the situation. Ask others how they experienced you. Reframe, through your ID, how you could have navigated that situation differently.

VII. USE YOUR idWORD TO LIVE INTO YOUR GREATNESS: You are made different to make a difference. We have used that phrase or some version of it 19 times in this book. It is what we believe. Most people do not think in these terms. People, on average see themselves as just regular, normal, as nothing-too-outstanding-individuals, and are contented to be so. We disagree. Now that you know your ID, you can—and you have a responsibility to—walk into your greatness.

The next step in optimizing your 5% is to turn performance into practice. We adhere to the amended version of the old, "practice makes perfect" adage. Instead we believe "practice makes permanent." Practice takes time—time spent daily.

You've probably suffered from the quick-fix empty promise of a magic formula. Diet and exercise books that promise the pounds will melt away if you buy their prescribed program. Self help books that promise a new you in 90 days or less. We are promised that we can improve everything from our waistline to our memory retention to our self-esteem if we will only follow the program.

So, we understand if you picked up this book half expecting to see yet another quick-fix formula for success. Not so. We offer you something real—something permanent. We offer you the voyage of a lifetime.

We say "voyage" intentionally. A voyage is different from a trip, or even from a journey. A trip can be short or long, eventful or uneventful. A journey is longer, but it can be tedious. No, we invite you on a voyage—with images of high seas and salt air, exhilarating adventure with good companions, and even a little danger with the unexpected sprinkled in at times. The voyage to discover and unleash your I.D. will take as long as it takes you. It will be challenging. It will be fun and exciting. It will have surprises—and it will at the same time be familiar. But you will not go it alone.

We are your guides as well as fellow voyagers with you!

Now, we understand if you are thinking, "Wait, guys, I don't want to go on a voyage. Who's got the time? Can you please just get to the point?"

Well, think of it this way. You are a complicated creature. Because of that, understanding the uniqueness of you takes time, thought, and reflection. But, we promise you, continue on this voyage with us and you will see yourself in an entirely new light.

You'll start to see yourself and your work, the things you love and the things that motivate you, in a life-transforming way.

Take the story of celebrated photographer, Chris Orwig, for example:

"Do you know what I mean when I say 'gutter palms'?" Chris asked us.

We were at his art studio in downtown Santa Barbara, surrounded by photographs by the likes of Rodney Smith, worth tens of thousands of dollars, and he was talking to us about 'gutter palms.'

"They are these tiny palm trees, growing because a seed had somehow found its way into a sidewalk crack. And against all the odds the little trees grew, emerging from the crack and pushing upwards towards the light. I realize in my life I am like a gutter palm—reaching for the light."

When Chris was in his twenties, he was battling an unexplained medical condition that resulted in chronic, debilitating pain and immobility. The farthest he could walk without a wheelchair was the length of a grocery store aisle. Add to this the fact that he had just recently walked away from school with one semester remaining to complete his master's degree. He was floundering. This was a difficult and dark time in his life. So you'll understand he was seriously depressed and wondering what sort of future lay ahead of him.

It was at that moment his father put a camera into his hand and everything changed. Or did it? The fact is, that simple gift unleashed something that was always in Chris. It was there all along, it just needed to be let out, explored, and optimized. Chris put what was different about him into intentional use, tapped into what was already there and what came forth was an explosion of clarity. "Photography became for me a way to get my focus off of myself at a time when I was very self-focused," he told us. "And the fact is it is still that today. The camera changed the way I look at everything. It showed me life is something to be savored, not just endured."

There was always something remarkable about Chris. Knowing him before he was a famous photographer, much less a sought-after teacher and mentor, you would have seen him as a regular guy. A fun-loving, adventurous, surfer, he played sports all throughout childhood and high school. Nothing about him touched on photography—or any of the visual arts. Nothing, except for a quiet unsettling whisper beneath the surface occasionally bubbling up when he would bring home a childhood masterpiece to his mom. He recalls, "The best lie my mom ever told me was there is no such thing as bad art." So you would see his house as a child decorated in art, his and his brother and sister. He tapped into his difference and applied intentionality, which brought him to life!

"My dad putting that camera in my hand started me on a voyage of discovery," Chris says now, looking back. "It triggered my discovery of what is uniquely different about me. I see beyond the image. I capture each person's story with my photos. So, when you guys speak of being intentional with your difference, I know that experientially. It is what I teach my students—to discover their uniqueness and bring that to their photography."

"The discovery of my unique difference is why I am here today doing what I do. In fact it brought about my healing. Soon after I started taking pictures, my unexplained, undiagnosed symptoms faded. I regained strength in my legs, my pain went away, and I am back to mountain climbing and running today."

With tears in his eyes, Chris turned to us and said, "This is very cool, this process that you do, helping people—me—discover a way to own, to articulate what is different about me. It's very powerful."

Stay the course and this will be powerful for you too—for your lifetime. For you to have this kind of life-impacting experience you must turn performance into practice. To turn your performance into permanent

See Chris Orwig's video
http://bit.ly/14eLur5

behavior you can, go online at www.intentionaldifference.me to sign up for our idMindmap™ online tool.

Or, you can just continue to read on. To turn performance into practice, to make your idWord yours, start by doing the following:

I. EXPLAIN YOUR ID TO OTHERS: In our observation one of the first things that people want to do upon discovering their idWord is to help others come to know their idWord. To do this you need to be able to tell them in a simple and clear way of your own discovery. To help you with this finish the sentence below:

I am (insert your idWord in the blank), _____ by that I mean, (finish the sentence by filling in the blank) _____.

For example: I am Catalyst, by that I mean, I come alongside individuals and organizations to launch new ideas.

II. PUT ID TO WORK IN YOUR DAILY LIFE: Remember how you came to your one word? No one gave it to you. You named the word yourself. It came to you through the process of identifying the following: the outcome(s) you are known for; your demonstrated passion; your indelible experiences; your acquired knowledge; your rehearsed skills; and your unique pattern of thinking, feeling, and behaving. It is your multi-dimensional identity. You have been living your difference for most of your life, automatically. What changes everything is you will now be intentional with your difference. So here are some ways to live your ID daily:

1. WORK YOUR IDWORD INTO YOUR DAILY INTERACTIONS. Force yourself to describe what you do best through that word. Then offer people an explanation. Maybe even add your idWord to your email signature line.

2. BECOME A FUTURE HISTORIAN WITH YOUR idWORD. In three to five, maybe even ten years from now, how do you want to embody your idWord? Record some thoughts, actions, behaviors, and perspectives you want to begin intentionally living into.

3. BUILD YOUR idPORTFOLIO™. Collect artifacts (events, interactions, photos, writings, etc.) that demonstrate and record your idWord in action.

4. ENLIST AN idCOACH™ OR idBUDDY™. Hire a certified idCoach or recruit a friend who will become a partner with you in helping you grow your Intentional Difference.

5. RECORD YOUR DISCOVERIES. Make daily journal entries in your idMindmap™ online.

Thank you for being fellow travelers with us. We faced some squalls, a few rough seas here and there, some unexpected reefs and sandbars, met some exotic natives, and made some great friends. But one last thing, friends. We totally respect the contributions of George Koehler, Michael Jordan's one-time chauffeur and long-time confidante.

We come back, over and over again, to one special thing he said. Remember this?

"I've met just about every one under the sun through Michael. If you picked up a book about Michael's life, it would be my life, just Michael's name on the cover."

George, it *is* YOUR life—a life lived well because you figured out who you had been made to be, so you could make a difference.

And the same can be and, we trust, WILL be true for you.

Your Intentional Difference is the unique fingerprint of your soul. It confirms your identity, validates your presence, and testifies of your purpose. It is the signature-song of your personality—whose melodious chorus reassuringly echoes to you and heralds out to the world, …"I AM, I AM, *I… AM.*"

So, we leave you. Momentarily. Not at the end of a journey. But rather, on a voyage with daily discoveries about what it means to be fully and intentionally YOU!

We look forward to traveling with you again soon.

Godspeed and fair winds!

What's Your ID

TOOLS TO HELP YOU CONTINUE YOUR VOYAGE

Intentional Difference Tools

The ID suite of tools increases individual and team productivity, organizational performance, and leadership effectiveness. Our ID tools include:

idDiscover
idExperience
idTransform
idOrganization
idTeam
idMatch
idAlignment
idUniversity

Individual Tools

idDiscover™

An in-person, online or virtual process individualized to you.

Through this process, people discover their idWord. This hour-long session engages the process of self discovery to help you discover and articulate your Intentional Difference in one word. This discovery is the foundation upon which you can now begin to live and work more daily within your 5% zone.

idDiscover creates a gestalt moment, where someone sees themselves, the world, and their place in the world in a fundamentally different and profound way. Because of this "identiological" reframe each individual begins to function with more intentionality and less on automatic pilot in their relationships, work and life.

Organizational Tools

idExperience™

A series of speeches or workshop events that invite participants into an interactive discovery of the six dimensions that make up Intentional Difference.

Level One: Intentional Difference: 1-hour dynamic and interactive, instructional speech with humor, anecdotes, case stories of others who have discovered their idWord and how the discovery has improved their work performance and relationships.

Level Two: Your Intentional Difference Leadership: 1-day deep dive into how your ID positions you to lead and succeed. Participants discover their idWord, and apply the six dimensions of ID by working in pairs and groups.

Level Three: Your Intentional Team. Just as individuals prior to discovery of their ID tend to operate on automatic pilot, so do teams. This 3-day interactive workshop teaches teams how to unleash the combined creative and productive power of each member being intentional with their difference. Participants discover their idWord. Receive a graphical illustration of how their ID impacts their contribution on a team. Each person receives an idAlignment report(see full description later in this list of products).

idTransform™

A coaching protocol that focuses on optimizing your leadership performance by using the lens of ID as a coaching tool.

This coaching partnership with a certified idCoach establishes metrics that facilitate the creation and execution of concrete performance goals.

This has a direct impact upon employee engagement, employee discretionary effort, employee retention, increased leadership effectiveness and improved job performance by helping you leverage your Intentional Difference.

idOrganization™

An idOrganization hires you to be you, to do this the idea of a 'manager' changes. Why? Because an idOrganization is built on the premise that people who know their ID manage themselves FIRST. And, they manage themselves more effectively than anyone else can. This idea changes the practice of management in an organizaton which in our experience, improves creativity, productivity and ownership by employees. This approach has proven to be especially valuable in multi-generational organizations. In this 6 hour session, each manager will:

- Identify and articulate their idWord
- Learn and begin to practice the 4 Keys to Managing with Your ID
- Be assigned an idCoach

Additionally, Building the idOrganization teaches managers how to help employees to use their ID:

1. to increase personal ownership in the organization
2. to increase individual contribution in their role
3. to decrease dependency upon managers
4. to decrease potential personality clashes

idTeam™

We believe that at the core good leadership starts with YOU. We believe that the best teams are made up of people who know WHO they are and use that "identiological" knowledge to facilitate the optimization of their team. We also believe that knowledge coupled with experience is the best teacher and ensures improved assimilation of data, which leads to behavior modification, team transformation and performance optimization.

Purpose: Helping teams optimize their Intentional Difference (ID).

Core Principles of idTeam

- Each individual can learn to optimize their ID.
- A team environment can help or inhibit a person from optimizing their ID.
- Teams that know, understand, and celebrate each person's ID are likely to experience improved communication, increased employee engagement, enhanced productivity and greater creativity.

- The key to these performance outcomes is helping the team unleash each individual's ID.

Methodology

Using our idMindMap© protocol, an idCoach guides team members through "mapping points." Team members are asked to reflect on their lives and develop their individual idMindMap "voyage."

This process of reflection both looks back (for context) and forward (for goal-setting) and enables the team member to see where they have and have not been intentional around their difference. The idCoach partners with each team member to lead, reflect back on the idDiscover learning, and ensure that the idMindMap is done through the lens of ID.

Additionally, because this is done in a participatory, team environment, it enables other team members to speak into the individual idMindMapping process, thus reducing the tendency for any one team member to fall prey to the "blind spot."

idMatch™

Beyond a candidate's resume there are specific traits needed for an individual to be the right fit and perform optimally in a specific role. The idMatch process allows you to identify that right hire by doing the following:

1. Identifying the critical functions and activities of the position to be filled.
2. Developing questions that identify the candidates' unique differences.
3. Assessing the match between each individual's unique differences and the critical activities of specific roles.
4. Teaching interviewers how to use the developed questions

5. Certifying each interviewer's level accuracy at a 95% rate
6. Unpacking the hiring interview and discussing selection of the person for the position.
7. Providing insight on how best to motivate, develop and focus the new hire. Developing metrics for the new hire's performance, to be assessed and reviewed six months into the job.

Benefits
1. Increased performance within a role
2. Increased productivity
3. Increased capacity for excellence
4. Increased employee role attachment
5. Increased retention

idAlignment™

We know that 85% of what we do most people can do. 10% of what we do some people can do or be trained to do. 5% of what we do we alone can do it or do it in the way we do it. This is our Flow Zone, this is where our Intentional Difference is optimized. idAlignment helps an individual align their present job within the context of their unique 5% zone.

How does it work?

Beyond each individual's resume there are specific traits needed to be the right fit and perform optimally in a specific role. The idAlignment process allows each team member to identify how their ID impacts your Critical Outcome, Critical Activities and Critical Emotions within their present job function by doing the following:

1. Identifying the critical functions and activities of their position.
2. Assessing the match between each individual's unique difference and the critical activities of their specific role.

3. Assessing the match between each individual's unique difference and the unique differences of the supervisor and peers in that specific role.
4. Assessing the pertinent emotions present and active within the specific role.
5. Assessing the match between each individual's unique difference and the culture of their organization.
6. Providing insight on how to best unleash, develop and apply ID to their role.
7. Developing metrics and milestones for performance, to be assessed and reviewed six months into the job.

Academic Tools

idUniversity™
The Numbers don't lie.

80% of college students do not know what they want to do when they get to college

75% of enrolled college students change their major at least twice

50% of college students change their major three to five times

Only half of first-time college students get a degree within six years, the rest take longer

Are college students this indecisive?

We believe that each student can achieve successful college outcomes when they are living from their Intentional Difference because each student is… Made different to make a difference! When you leverage the energy of each student's unique difference (instead of viewing their difference as a deficit), their educational performance improves!

We help students and educational organizations achieve extraordinary performance by teaching each individual how to harness their difference. Our suite of customizable tools enables each person to discover and apply their Intentional Difference at anytime during matriculation.

idBehavior ™
Your ID: Your Impact

idBehavior builds and re-inforces self-esteem in elementary, high school and college students. This module is delivered online through a "blackboard" type platform that allows for interaction, collaboration and learning events between students, parents, teachers and mentors.

Intentional Difference provides a disciplined approach to identifying and understanding the six dimensions that make up our Intentional Difference and how they impact and drive personal relationships. The idBehavior module specifically takes a student's understanding of their own difference, and those of others around the student, to a level where self-esteem is improved by the intentional leverage of one's innate differences, addressing some of the imbalance of perceived power as in the case of bullying.

ABOUT THE AUTHORS

Ken Tucker is a highly sought after speaker, thought leader, trusted advisor, and chief designer of the *Intentional Difference Process*. He has authored or co-authored 4 books. A former Gallup Organization consultant and Keynote Speaker, Ken is now a Senior Partner at TAG. In his role at TAG, Ken serves as a leadership strategist and executive coach for chief officers in Fortune 500 companies and Government Agencies in the US, Mexico, United Kingdom and Australia. Ken has been interviewed by Sam Donaldson, appeared on Bloomberg Television. Ken has shared speaking platforms with Colin Powell, Jim Collins and Marcus Buckingham. Ken and his family live in Virginia and Florida.

Todd Hahn is a business leader, not-for-profit executive, executive coach for Fortune 500 and mid-sized companies, and church pastor. He has authored/co-authored four books, and is recognized internationally as a thought leader on generational transformation and as a subject matter expert in helping organizations become incubators of creativity and industry leaders. His passion is to help leaders master their strengths in order to become all they can be. Hahn lives with his family in Charlotte, NC.

Shane Roberson is a cultural architect, transformational coach and a catalyst. He serves as Vice President for Client Services with The Armstrong Group (TAG). In his role he serves as a cultural strategist and executive coach for chief officers in healthcare, federal government agencies, and Fortune 500 companies. His passion is to bring out the best in people, assisting them to become the best for the world and optimizing organizational and team performance. He is an avid runner, a speaker, and a lifelong student of people. Shane lives in Richmond, Virginia with his wife, Jennifer and their three daughters, Jessica, Amanda and Emma.

THE LEADERSHIP TRIANGLE
Introduction

This is a book about leadership, but it may be unlike any leadership book you have ever read! Together, we are going to challenge some common assumptions about what leadership is and how you can practice it. You are going to receive some new tools that will help you to lead effectively in even the most challenging environments. You'll be challenged to rethink much of what you have been taught about leadership in the past. And you'll be stretched to dream of the long-term, positive impact you can make in your world!

This is a book for leaders of all types, regardless of position or industry. It is for business leaders, to be sure. But it is also for teachers, coaches, pastors, chairpersons of not-for-profit boards, and even parents. If you lead at any level in your life, this book is for you.

In our work as consultants and thought leaders we are around a lot of leaders. It is our privilege to coach, counsel and advise leaders and soon-to-be leaders from all sorts of industries in all sorts of settings.

We've learned a lot and we continue to learn more every day. We've discovered along the way that leadership is a journey and we are excited about sharing this leg of the journey with you.

We are excited to share with you three gifts in this book, gifts we have benefited from immensely ourselves and that continue to sharpen our own leadership.

We offer you the gift of personal interactions with some of the world's greatest leaders. We have had the chance to spend time with some amazing leaders and we draw on those experiences in this book. Leaders like Truett Cathey, the founder of Chick-fil-A. Ken Blanchard, the famous author and speaker. Frances Hesselbein, leader of the Drucker Institute. Steve Reinemund, the former head of Pepsi and now an esteemed business school dean. British business guru, Charles Handy. Pete Coors, of Molson-Coors Brewing Company. And Tom Cousins, the legendary business executive who led perhaps the most remarkable transformation of an at-risk community in American history. In fact, the first couple of chapters of this book will dig deep into that story, the Miracle at East Lake.

But this is not just about well-known people and grandiose stories of change. We will also share the gift that we've been given as we interact with ordinary people. Middle managers with government jobs. Pastors of small churches. Executives in corporate America. Volunteers in non-profit organizations. What we have learned from them has changed our view of the world.

We offer you the gift of many practical tools that you can begin to use today— right now! These tools will immediately improve your leadership skills.

We have one more gift we would like to offer you—the gift of a Triangle that has shaped and reshaped our understanding of leadership.

At the core of the Leadership Triangle is the belief that different kinds of leadership challenges call for different types of *Leadership*

Options—choices the leader can make. We are passionate about helping you identify what sort of challenges you as a leader are facing and then choosing the right Option to deal with them. We believe that if you understand and, more important, act within this framework then your effectiveness as a leader will be multiplied many times.

We are honored that you have chosen to spend this time with us, reading our book and running this leg of the leadership journey along with us. Here's to our growth and effectiveness as leaders! Let us introduce you to one of the most compelling leadership stories we've ever encountered. Are you ready to dig in?

CHAPTER ONE

A LETTER
AND PHONE CALL
Not Your Average Phone Call

I turned up the volume up for the third time, trying to absorb what I was watching. I was in a hotel room, somewhere on a client trip, probably in Seattle, when I saw Tom. An old family friend. On late night TV. Why was Tom on TV?

I remember swimming in his pool when I was four years old. Seeing him at dinner last summer in the mountains. He had never been one for the limelight, but here he was on national TV.

That same night, in a different city, Warren turned on the same news segment. We were miles apart. Tom was in Atlanta. Warren was in Omaha. And I think I was in Seattle. But that news segment crossed general boundaries and time zones in ways that had far-reaching implications.

I've never met Warren and doubt that I ever will. But Tom and Warren had known each other for many years and considered each other allies and even friends. But Warren had never heard about a project in Atlanta that Tom was finishing. A project that very few people believed in. A project designed to transform one of the worst neighborhoods in the city, a place the locals called "Little Vietnam." And here was Tom, on national TV, talking about that project. I turned up the volume once more, fully engaged even though my body said it was 2:00 a.m.

The neighborhood was called East Lake. It had a storied past, including the distinction of being the location of the golf course called home by the legendary golfer Bobby Jones. It was a resort where Atlanta's well-heeled had socialized, cut business deals, and sipped single malt Scotch at the nineteenth hole.

But that was decades ago. A public housing project—East Lake Meadows had been erected in East Lake decades later. Over the years, the project had become known for its violent crime and drug culture. By the mid-1990s, if you had the courage to take a drive through the littered streets of East Lake Meadows, you would see the tawdriest of landscapes.

The grassless yards scattered with debris. The ramshackle houses, most with boarded windows and sagging porches—they all had the unmistakable look and smell of decay.

Some residents never came out of their homes, terrified of the streets. Other residents, sullen of expression and with eyes forlorn of light, roamed the streets like vagabond kings. You would see men exchanging crumpled wads of cash for dime bags, out in broad daylight.

Tom had mastered the facts about East Lake Meadows. Facts that painted an almost inconceivable portrait of pain and hopelessness. A sky high crime rate, possibly Georgia's highest. A mortality rate that sounded like an impoverished African nation. An impossibly high rate of births to unwed teenage mothers. Almost endemic illiteracy.

But Tom was a stubborn man—all of his friends said so. He was determined that this sort of place should not exist in his city, not in Atlanta. And he was determined that he was going to be a part of turning it around. He knew that if the transformation were to happen it would take way more than one man's determined efforts. It would take a team—a tough, talented, devoted team. A stubborn team.

He started dreaming dreams, rattling cages and enlisting supporters and leaders. He started describing his dreams and meeting with almost uniform disbelief and derision.

"East Lake Meadows?!" they would say. "The worst place in the country? All you will be doing is throwing good money after bad and wasting your time in the bargain. Forget it, Tom. It can't be done."

He knew they had a point or two. The problems in East Lake Meadows were not simple ones; they were ones that would require change at the most fundamental level. Where would such an effort even start? With crime reduction, education, drug treatment, or with economic revitalization? How many people—politicians and Tenants Association leaders, government bureaucrats, real estate developers looking to turn a buck—would have to work together for a common purpose? This was going to be a monumental challenge.

Fifteen years after the project started, but only a few days after the TV show aired on CNBC, Tom got Warren's letter. It came from halfway across the country and it was simple. I saw a television program on what you are doing there in Atlanta. I think it just might work in other places. If you need anything, I have access to resources. Just call me and let me know.

So Tom did call, even before putting the letter down. "Warren," he said, "thanks for your letter. I would like your help. I don't need your money for East Lake. But I would like your help in replicating this model in other cities."

That ten minute television segment started us down the path of thinking about the Leadership Triangle. It formed a backdrop for how we, at TAG

Consulting, think about leadership. It was part of what drew Ken Tucker to join our consulting practice and to co-author this book with me.

And that ten minute television segment was the impetus for Warren Buffett to join Tom Cousins in trying to change the world.

Transformation at East Lake Meadows

When it comes to leadership we can all agree on one thing: it is not easy!

The world moves at a screamingly fast pace, demanding lightning fast response times and decisions made on the fly. A fundamentally changing economy means that long taken-for-granted ground rules are out the window and the "new normal" isn't always clear. Social media has transformed the way organizations of all kinds communicate with their constituencies and customers. The traditional rules governing production and distribution of goods and services have given way to a new order where consumers are also producers.

This complexity affects organizations of all types—in the for-profit, not-for-profit, and public sectors. For-profits must compete with fast-rising economies in other parts of the world and navigate industries which seem to change overnight. Not-for-profits must contend with often aging donor bases and increased competition for dollars from the public and private sectors. And political pundits wonder openly if the United States is even governable anymore.

And we have to lead in the middle of all this complexity! If you have been leading a group for any length of time we bet you have found that time-tested methods of leadership don't seem to be working as well as they used to.

The most pressing leadership question of the moment is not just about profits or growth or shareholder value or market share. It is: "What does it mean to lead in such a way that my team or organization can adapt, compete, and thrive at levels beyond the surface?" This is the case whether you are leading a business, a department, a volunteer board, or a church committee.

This is the challenge that Tom Cousins and his team faced at East Lake Meadows in Atlanta.

East Lake had once been legacy ground for Bobby Jones, regarded as one of the greatest and unquestionably the most important golfer of all time. Jones won championship after championship without relinquishing his amateur status, foregoing paychecks for a pure love of the game. He battled a debilitating disease that would have robbed the spirits of many a lesser man. He founded the legendary Augusta National Golf Club where every spring the most prestigious professional tournament in America, the Masters, is played.

So it makes sense that the place where Bobby Jones played his first and last round would be hallowed ground for lovers of the game everywhere. And it made it all the more sad when this site, the East Lake Country Club in Atlanta, Georgia, had fallen into disrepair in the 1970s. Once lush fairways were patchy and browning. Greens were worn and diseased. Formerly lush tee boxes offered bare spots that promised to snap tees in two.

But the golf course was the least of the East Lake area's problems. Once a haven for the well-heeled of Atlanta to socialize, golf, consummate business deals, and sip cocktails, a half century of wear and tear and the city's growth in other directions meant that East Lake had lost its luster by the 1960s. And then came the fateful decision to build a public housing project in East Lake on the site of the Number Two golf course.

East Lake Meadows was in trouble from the start. Its 650 units were home to some of the most desperately poor residents in the United States. Poverty led to hopelessness, which led to a desire to escape, which led to drugs and alcohol, which led to crime, which led to cycles of gruesome violence.

Residents kept their blinds drawn even during the daytime. Every neighbor had a story of seeing a mugging or a shooting or a robbery. Atlantans called the East Lake area "Little Vietnam" and stayed away in droves. Police simply called East Lake Meadows a "war zone."

By 1995, East Lake Meadows was one of the poorest, most violent communities in the nation. The crime rate was eighteen times the national average. The employment rate (not the UNemployment rate, mind you) was at 14 percent. The average age of a grandmother in East Lake Meadows was thirty-two. That's right. Thirty-two.

East Lake Meadows was a desperately poor, desperately despised area, forgotten by its city, largely ignored by its city's leaders. A place of problems both systemic and individual. A place without hope. Until a wealthy sixty-something developer with a passion for golf picked up the *New York Times* one day.

A Fast Rise To The Top

Tom Cousins, entrepreneur and successful businessman, moved to Atlanta in 1954. His first job was respectable but hardly indicative of the career that was to come. He parlayed that initial job with a company that manufactured kits for homebuilders into a home building company of his own. By the early 1960s, Cousins was the largest homebuilder in the state of Georgia. In the mid-1960s he got into commercial and office development and his success grew exponentially.

Cousins' resume is nothing short of stunning. This onetime pre-med student who nearly fainted the first time he witnessed a surgical procedure was largely responsible for transforming downtown Atlanta in the 1980s. He developed the CNN Center, 191 Peachtree Tower, and built the largest skyscraper in the nation outside of Chicago and New York City. He organized and chaired Atlanta's Billy Graham Crusade. Cousins donated the land for the Georgia World Congress Center. He brought pro basketball (the Atlanta Hawks) and major league hockey (the Atlanta Flames, now the Calgary Flames) to the city. When his basketball team needed a larger arena, he built the Omni which at the time was a state of the art sports complex.

An innately humble man, Cousins enjoyed social prestige, political influence, and immense wealth. He had plenty of time to play his beloved game of golf, along with a passionate desire to help others. Life was good and his had been well lived. But then one day he picked up the *New York Times* and began the journey that would lead him to the greatest challenge of his career—being part of the team that would lead the transformation of East Lake Meadows.

The NYT article pointed out that the vast majority of inmates in New York's state prison system were from a small handful of neighborhoods— no more than eight. Cousins told us that he reasoned the same must be true in Georgia. So he asked Atlanta's chief of police. "Sure, Tom, everyone knows that," said the Chief. Only, in Georgia, 75 percent of the prison population comes out of maybe five neighborhoods in Atlanta alone. And most of those come out of ONE neighborhood—East Lake. "Little Vietnam. One of the worst places in the world."

Cousins had heard of East Lake Meadows but he decided to ask around. What he found stunned him. But the true day of reckoning was when he braved a field trip to the project itself. "I could not believe this was a place in America," he told us later, shaking his head.

When he began talking about his hopes to transform the area, his friends and other Atlanta leaders began shaking *their* heads. The problems are too deep and severe, he was told. That would be throwing good money after bad, they said. We'd be better off to tear the place down and start over or maybe just wall the whole neighborhood off, some argued. Most daunting of all, the people living in the community will never trust you, some said convincingly.

But Cousins was tenacious by nature and gripped by a growing vision to break the cycle of poverty and despair in East Lake Meadows.

And golf—of all games, the game of the wealthy elite—provided him an entry point.

Cousins loved the game of golf and was a very good player. Once, while playing with the legendary pro golfer Jack Nicklaus in a Pro-Am event, Cousins was actually leading Nicklaus as they prepared to tee off on the seventeenth hole. Nicklaus looked at Cousins and said, "Tom, have you ever considered joining us on the professional tour?" Cousins promptly hit his next shot, sending the ball directly into a lake. Later, Cousins asked Nicklaus if the golfer had been trying to get in his head and Nicklaus just smiled.

But beyond playing and enjoying the game himself, Cousins saw that golf could be leveraged for a bigger purpose. So he set his sights on the East Lake Club.

Threadbare and unable to attract golfers because of the neighboring war zone, East Lake Golf Club was struggling. Disputes between the private partners who owned the course had ended up in court and the judge had ordered them to sell the Club. Tom Cousins paid the price himself—twenty-five million dollars—and hatched an ingenious plan.

If he could convince one hundred new corporate members to sign up for the club, paying an initiation fee of $50,000 and making a suggested donation of $200,000 to the East Lake Foundation he would leverage the resources of the Cousins Family Foundation to renovate the golf club. Of the first one hundred, $200,000 donations half would go to support the community programs of the East Lake Foundation and half was paid to the Cousins Family Foundation to offset the renovation and other costs. After that, all of the remaining $200,000 and any future profits from the East Lake Golf Club would be returned to the East Lake Foundation (this continues today and, in addition, all profits from the PGA TOUR Championship event held at the club go to the foundation). A natural salesman and a deeply convincing man, Cousins got the members he needed. But the climb up the mountain had just begun. Tom Cousins would need all the resources of his vast experience, network of contacts, and sustaining Christian faith to make it to the top.

For one thing, Cousins' vision was not just about East Lake. From the outset, he envisioned that what happened in East Lake would point the way to a transferable model which could be taken to similar communities across the nation.

Cousins faced a task that would have intimidated a lesser leader. He had come to the end of his ability—by himself—to create change. Now, he had to form a series of alliances with individuals and groups who usually viewed their interests and values as in conflict. He had to convince them to cast aside personal agendas, deep-seated distrust, and even personal security to work together to accomplish a seemingly impossible task. The change East Lake Meadows needed was not incremental, but rather transformational. A whole new community was to be created, shaped by people behaving in ways very unusual for them.

First would be the residents themselves. Battered by crime, poverty, disease, and shattered families, the good-hearted residents of East Lake Meadows would have to believe—and act on the belief—that this plan initiated by outsiders would work and would be in their best interests. Most dramatically, they would have to move out of their homes for a time so that the community could be rebuilt, having only Tom Cousins' word for a guarantee that they would be welcomed back.

Things did not go well initially. A local leader told Eva Davis, the formidable head of the neighborhood association, that Cousins was "sneaky" and should bear watching. Eva Davis had stymied former President Jimmy Carter not too long ago. She wasn't afraid of a real estate developer. Not one to be fooled easily, Eva refused to cooperate until she had reason to trust.

But even if Cousins could convince the residents of East Lake Meadows to go along, he still had to run a gamut. He would have to create a public-private partnership like Atlanta had never seen. Businesses and financial institutions would have to inject large amounts of capital into a never-before-proven idea. Political leaders would have to cooperate with housing and zoning variances and do the thing that politicians loathe to do—spend political capital.

This is a theme that we come back to again and again in the East Lake story—no one person could make the change needed alone. People were going to have to be persuaded to behave in surprising ways, ways that might at first appear to go against their self-interest.

Behaving In Unpredictable Ways

That was just the thing, Cousins soon realized. People were going to have to do things that were the precise opposite of what they would normally be inclined to do. Residents who trusted no one would have to trust strangers. Individuals with cash who normally required a great return on investment and lots of guarantees would have to risk it all. And political leaders skilled at minimizing risk, and playing the angles in their own favor would have to act selflessly. So Tom Cousins began to paint a vision and woo a city. In so doing, he created a masterpiece of leadership that is a guiding narrative of *The Leadership Triangle*.

He had always believed in bringing people together to accomplish common goals. Once, in the early 1960s Cousins had led an initiative to bring African-American and white leaders together. At one meeting, Cousins was seated across from Dr. Martin Luther King, Jr. At one point during the meeting King, Jr., who was just becoming prominent, turned to Cousins and said, "What do you think of me?" Cousins smiled and replied, "I hear you are a rabble rouser and a law breaker!" King, Jr. laughed and said, "Yes, that's right, but I am willing to pay the price." So was Tom Cousins.

Cousins and his team were forced to operate at an extraordinarily high level to meet such a wide range of challenges. He had to navigate very specific and complex tactical obstacles that required great expertise and skill. He had to understand the external environment and formulate a strategy that would succeed in the face of opposition and long odds. He had to create alignment among groups that at times saw themselves in fundamental opposition to one another.

And, most challenging of all, the team had to transform values, which involved the essential and often agonizing work of exposing the existing values of all the involved parties—values that were often in conflict.

Those are the things that truly transformational leaders do. And, we will see, these are the things that **you** can do whether you are a businessperson, head of a not-for-profit or a volunteer organization, or leader of a church. The challenges that faced East Lake and Tom Cousins were unique—as are yours—but the principles of the leadership triangle which he practiced are universal.

So, what was the vision Cousins painted as he sought to persuade across tables in corporate boardrooms, restaurants fancy and plain, the mansions in Buckhead and the broken down homes of East Lake Meadows?

A New Foundation, A New Dream

In Tom Cousins' imagination East Lake Meadows would be a model community, full of hard-working, law-abiding citizens who looked out for one another. The residents would be a testament to the belief— the fact—that predictable cycles of poverty, crime and despair are not inevitable.

To help make the vision a reality, Cousins plowed his own money into a new organization—the East Lake Foundation—designed to provide common ground to the diverse parties who were necessary to the project. The Foundation's goal was to "help transform the East Lake neighborhood and create new opportunities for the families that live there." Community "redevelopment" was a common phrase in 1995. The East Lake vision was more about community re-creation.

The project would require participation—to greater and lesser degrees—from a wide range of players. There were public partners (the Atlanta Housing Authority, the Atlanta Public Schools, and a critical grant from the U.S. government), private partners (Emory University, Oglethorpe University, the Publix grocery store chain, the YMCA) and financial partners (SunTrust and Wells Fargo banks).At the outset, in the middle, and towards the end of the project, each of these entities would play a role. Most important of all, there were the residential partners in East Lake Meadows itself.

And there were individual leaders whom Cousins recruited to the cause— successful men and women from academia, the marketplace, the legal profession—all of whom subordinated their egos and risked their reputations to enlist against daunting odds. People like, Renee Glover, Madelyn Adams, Charlie Harrison, Don Edwards, Lillian and Greg Giornelli, Carol Naughton, Chuck Knapp, and the eventual mayor of Atlanta, Shirley Franklin. You will meet many of them in this book.

The once skeptical Eva Davis began to spend time with Cousins and his family and, in her own words, "came to love them." Traditional economic and racial boundaries began to dissolve as she saw that he really cared about her neighborhood and its people and, significantly, had the power and influence to actually bring change. Eva Davis began to leverage her influence to do the unthinkable—persuade her neighbors to move into temporary housing so that the dilapidated buildings of East Lake Meadows could be transformed into the Villages of East Lake. And, slowly, the transformation began to happen.

In this book, we will share many stories that illustrate how Tom Cousins, his colleagues, and many other leaders exemplified the principles of the Leadership Triangle. But, for now, let's just capture a snapshot view of East Lake in 2011.

East Lake Meadows is now the Villages of East Lake, with 542 mixed income housing units. Half of the units are reserved for families who receive public assistance, and nearly all of those families have heads of household who are either working or receiving job training. The other half of the units are reserved for middle income families.

The broader East Lake Community includes the Charles R. Drew Charter School, Atlanta's first charter school which has 800 students in pre-kindergarten through eighth grade. In 2010 at Drew, 96 percent of the students met or exceeded state requirements for reading and 91 percent did so for math.

There is Sheltering Arms Early Education and Family Center, providing care for kids from birth to kindergarten. There is a pristine East Lake Family YMCA and a well-stocked Publix grocery store.

Violent crime is down a staggering 95 percent. The percentage of residents on welfare has declined from 58 percent to 5 percent. The employment rate for those receiving public assistance has skyrocketed from 14-71 percent.

A Crucial Link

And there is golf. The prestigious PGA TOUR Championship is held on the Rees Jones-redesigned East Lake Golf Club, but that is not the most important "golf" thing.

East Lake is the home to the "First Tee of East Lake program," a rapidly expanding effort to leverage the beauty of the game of golf to mentor and shape at- risk youngsters. Sponsored by the World Foundation of Golf, First Tee uses the lessons of golf to teach participants "life-affirming" values such as honesty, integrity, commitment, and excellence.

Those values are part of the reason Tom Cousins loves golf so much. He sees in the game a unique emphasis on personal accountability and moral character, talents or traits that dovetail with his deep Christian faith and the way he has lived his life. In East Lake golf, the most "elite" of games, is helping at-risk kids learn values and patterns of behavior which will help them navigate the world outside the boundaries of East Lake.

East Lake, remember, is where the world's most important golfer—Bobby Jones—played his first and last rounds. It is a source of inspiration to Tom Cousins and to many others that East Lake today could be fostering other golfers who will play and live with excellence.

Beyond the Statistics, Stories

As we begin our journey of understanding the Leadership Triangle and how its principles can shape the way you lead in your own setting, we will look back to the East Lake story a few more times. We hope you will find it as encouraging and inspiring as we do. It is a story that offers instruction, for sure. But more important, it offers hope of transformation.

Perhaps Eva Davis puts it best...

"We tore down hell and replaced it with heaven!"

CPSIA information can be obtained at www.ICGtesting.com
Printed in the USA
BVOW08s2055180314

348035BV00003B/5/P